Witness Essentials

EVANGELISM THAT MAKES DISCIPLES

Daniel Meyer

IVP Connect

An imprint of InterVarsity Press
Downers Grove, Illinois

InterVarsity Press
P.O. Box 1400, Downers Grove, IL 60515-1426
World Wide Web: www.ivpress.com
E-mail: email@ivpress.com

InterVarsity Press® is the book-publishing division of InterVarsity Christian Fellowship/USA®, a movement of students and faculty active on campus at hundreds of universities, colleges and schools of nursing in the United States of America, and a member movement of the International Fellowship of Evangelical Students. For information about local and regional activities, write Public Relations Dept., InterVarsity Christian Fellowship/USA, 6400 Schroeder Rd., P.O. Box 7895, Madison, WI 53707-7895, or visit the IVCF website at <www.intervarsity.org>.

All Scripture quotations, unless otherwise indicated, are taken from the Holy Bible, New International Version®. NIV®. Copyright ©1973, 1978, 1984 by International Bible Society. Used by permission of Zondervan Publishing House. All rights reserved.

While all stories in this book are true, some names and identifying information in this book have been changed to protect the privacy of the individuals involved.

Cover design: Cindy Kiple
Interior design: Beth Hagenberg
Images: Old tree: David Sacks/Getty Images
Cosmic balloons: ©Pingebat/iStockphoto
Businessman on ladder: ©James Lee/iStockphoto
Money icons: ©Kathy Kankle/iStockphoto
Family icons: ©bubaone/iStockphoto

ISBN 978-0-8308-1089-5

Printed in the United States of America ∞

Library of Congress Cataloging-in-Publication Data

Meyer, Daniel, 1959-
Witness essentials: evangelism that makes disciples / Daniel
Meyer.
p. cm.
Includes bibliographical references.
ISBN 978-0-8308-1089-5 (pbk. : alk. paper)
1. Evangelistic work—Textbooks. I. Title.
BV3796.M49 2012
269'.2—dc23

2011051592

P	23	22	21	20	19	18	17	16	15	14	13	12	11	10	9	8	7	6	5	4	3	2	1
Y	31	30	29	28	27	26	25	24	23	22	21	20	19	18	17	16	15	14	13	12			

For my Savior and Lord, Jesus Christ,
whose gospel remains the best news I know

For my wife, Amy,
whose colorful witness I continually admire

For my sons, Rush, Cole and Reed,
in whom I pray God will bear his richest fruit

For my parents, Edward and Linda,
whose loving insistence set me in the way of Christ

For Mike Coffield,
who shared the invitation that led me into the kingdom

For those future disciples
whom God will bring to faith through you

Contents

A Word from the Author

In addition to those I have cited on the dedication page, I owe a debt of gratitude to many other persons whom God has used to advance his grace in and through me:

- To my first mentor in evangelism, Ben Johnson, and the other authors cited in this book who have inspired my thinking on this topic;
- To my colleague and friend, Greg Ogden, who graciously welcomed my contribution to the Essentials brand he pioneered;
- To the staff and congregation of Christ Church of Oak Brook who kindly allowed me the margin to work on this book, and especially my assistant, Deb Reha;
- To the mission partners of Christ Church whose practice of the essential elements of a faithful witness continues to inform me;
- To Tamara West, Noel Anderson, Paul Watermulder and the other kind friends who provided such helpful feedback in the fieldtesting of this book;
- And, finally, to that great cloud of witnesses (Hebrews 12:1) who have passed on the faith to all of us.

May this curriculum further "equip the saints for the work of ministry, for building up the body of Christ" (Ephesians 4:12 NRSV).

Soli Deo Gloria,
Daniel Meyer

Introduction
What Is Witness Essentials *About?*

You will receive power when the Holy Spirit comes on you;
and you will be my witnesses in Jerusalem, and in all
Judea and Samaria, and to the ends of the earth.

ACTS 1:8

WHERE ARE WE HAVING TROUBLE?

Some years ago, Christian leadership consultant Kent Hunter shared the results of a survey in which churchgoers were asked, "With which areas of the Christian life do you struggle most?" Here are the seven most frequently voiced answers in descending order:

7. Resisting temptation to immorality

6. Praying daily

5. Being a good family member

4. Loving everyone in a Christlike manner

3. Reading the Bible daily (or having a strong devotional life)

2. Seeking God's kingdom first, not worldly ways

1. Being a witness for Christ[1]

In other words, there are many dimensions of discipleship with which average Christians have difficulty. Those surveyed, however, said that their number one area of confusion or challenge is how to be a more effective or faithful witness to Jesus Christ.

On one level, the fact that witnessing ranked so highly on people's list of concerns is quite encouraging. Many Christians understand that Christ's final charge to his disciples was on this subject. They know that Jesus wanted his followers to draw many others into the life of the kingdom of God. The expansion of the early church was a dramatic fulfillment of this vision. The great missionary movements throughout history have been a further reflection of that mandate. The explosive growth of discipleship in many parts of the planet today reminds us that followers of Christ are still having this kind of life-changing influence.

In much of the Western world, however, Christian witness is obviously struggling. A lot of churches are shrinking. The credibility of the Christian message is sinking. A strategy for reversing these trends is absent from many Christians' thinking. This is puzzling. Why are the final and arguably most important instructions Jesus gave to his disciples before his ascension also the last ones that many Christians feel comfortable following?

WHY ARE WE STRUGGLING TO BE WITNESSES?

The answer to this question and the remedy to this problem is the focus of this book. To approach the challenge, however, let's consider some of the factors that may contribute to the current struggle. As I've listened to churchgoers talk through the years, several key themes repeatedly emerge:

- *The public speaking factor.* For many people, the call to be a witness for Christ immediately suggests the need to make a speech about theological matters. Repeated studies suggest that the prospect of public speaking ranks just ahead of going to school naked or dying a horrible death on the all-time fear list for most individuals. Given this reality, it isn't hard to see why a lot of people feel very anxious about the call to be a witness. *"Is there a way of being a witness that doesn't involve me standing up and speaking publicly about my faith?"*

- *The bad actor factor.* Compounding this tension is the fact that many of us have noticed the reception given to certain kinds of Christian witnesses. As Michael Simpson observes:

  > Evangelism as most people know it is an unnatural act. Christians knock on strangers' doors, interrupting their time with their family, stop random people in the street, divert vacationers' enjoyment, and flash Bible verses at sporting events. Others stand on street corners spouting the promise of eternal damnation at passersby with a white-knuckled grip on a well-worn Bible, which appears more as a weapon than a beacon of hope.[2]

  Even when we understand that this is not the only style of witness possible, the damage done by these "religious telemarketers" makes the thought of being a witness even more daunting for ordinary people. None of us wants to come across like the sort of voice that Caller ID and pop-up blockers were invented to screen out. *"I don't want to be viewed like one of those obnoxious people."*

- *The competency factor.* Underlying all of this is the fact that many Christians are not sure what they'd say or how they'd go about saying it if they actually got serious about witnessing. *"Where would I start? What would I say if I came up against an atheist or somebody with hard-core questions?"* Many Christians think, *It's better if I leave evan-*

gelism to the "gifted ones," the professional pastors and missionaries.

- *The terminology factor.* I've found that many people are also confused about the meaning of the words that swirl around this area of the Christian life. *"Is witness the same thing as evangelism? Is evangelism a component of witness or is witness a part of evangelism? What exactly* is *the gospel that I am supposed to share with others? How does all of this fit into the subject of discipleship? I don't know what all this terminology means."*

- *The priority-passion factor.* Hiding beneath the surface of some people's difficulty with witnessing is often a deeper sentiment: *"I don't think that my being a witness matters that much."* Some feel that their church or fellowship seems to be going along OK without their witnessing efforts. Those who occupy a shrinking circle may feel that it is too late to turn things around. While acknowledging some nagging uncertainty about the topic of hell, a lot of Christians seem to feel little passion for evangelism, or assign it a low priority compared to other spiritual activities.

- *The alternative ministry factor.* All of these factors lead many to invest their energies in ministry areas where they feel greater clarity, passion or prospect for success. Others simply try to get out to church more often, or brush up on the Bible, or use their time and talents to help out elsewhere. While bearing witness to Christ ranks at the top of the list of disciplines in which believers sense they ought to be better, many conclude: *"I'll just minister in other ways."*

WHAT'S YOUR INTEREST IN THIS SUBJECT?

The fact that you've picked up this book suggests that in spite of these factors, or perhaps because of them, the subject of Christian witness matters to you. Maybe you want it to become an even more vital part of your discipleship. Perhaps you are looking at this material because you are eager to equip others for this calling. Take a few moments to assess your place in this story.

1. As you survey the factors outlined in the section above, which ones do you recognize in your own experience or that of other Christians you know?

2. What other issues or dynamics do you believe prevent followers of Jesus today from being even more luminous representatives of the faith?

3. What particular questions about the subject of Christian witness do you hope will be addressed in the course of this study?

WHO IS THIS BOOK FOR?

All of the issues described thus far (and other issues we'll discuss in chapters ahead) spurred me to write this book. *Witness Essentials* is for anyone who has ever struggled with how to bear witness to Christ because of lack of vision, intention or means. It is for people who may feel that their own faith and discipleship needs a fresh start or a kick-start to move to a new level:

- *Students and young adults* who believe that the way of Jesus is beautiful and good but need help seeing how to live it out beyond the "God box" of a religious institution.

- *Other Christian laypeople* who want a deeper understanding of the message of Jesus, a better way of sharing their faith in him and a greater positive impact on the life of others.

- *Church or parachurch staff* who are looking for an enjoyable, biblical and practical tool to help themselves and the people they influence become more winsome witnesses of the life-changing love of Jesus Christ.

My goal is to help you and the other Christ-followers you may influence to (1) *grasp the gospel message* in its fullest meaning and implications; (2) *practice evangelism* in an attractive and respectful way; and (3) *advance life change* that blesses others and brings glory to God. Jesus has given his followers the most magnificent calling in history. It is now our time to answer it anew. Come join me in thinking further about what that means.

In What Contexts Might This Book Be Used?

Witness Essentials has a flexible format suitable for use in a variety of different individual, group and organizational settings. It will be of use to

- *An aspiring individual.* To guide the personal devotion and growth of someone seeking to further develop his or her capacity for influence.

- *A mentoring relationship.* To spark learning and discussion between a mentor and an apprentice.

- *A ministry team.* To help them (e.g., elders, church staff, evangelism or mission teams) clarify their calling and move on to greater impact.

- *A small group or Bible class.* To catalyze the thinking and practice of people interested in exerting greater influence for the kingdom of God.

- *A congregation.* To serve as the basis or supplemental resource for a sermon series that helps church members think about their role as Christian witnesses.

What's Included in Each Chapter of *Witness Essentials?*

Each chapter of this book contains five common elements:

- *Core Truth.* At the start of each lesson is a carefully crafted nugget of truth that summarizes some key aspect of the ministry of Christian witness in a catechetical (question and answer) format. The other four elements of each chapter simply expand on this core insight.

- *Memory Verse.* Throughout history, God's people have strengthened their witness by implanting his Word in their minds. For this reason, each lesson contains a verse or two that you are invited to commit to memory, along with some study questions to help you plumb the meaning of these wonderful texts.

- *Inductive Bible Study.* Each chapter also invites you to read a longer passage of Scripture that unpacks a key dimension of the core truth. The study questions will help you do some deeper Bible study, apply scriptural truth to your work as a witness and enhance your appreciation of the reading that follows.

- *Reading.* The reading included in each lesson develops the ideas presented in the core truth. Through a blend of storytelling, biblical illustrations and practical tips, you'll develop a richer understanding of Christian witness.

- *Application Exercise.* At the close of each chapter is an exercise that gives you the opportunity to distill the main points from the reading, identify some personal takeaways and reflect on how these insights or practices can improve your influence on the lives of others.

How Can I Adapt *Witness Essentials* for My Setting?

À la carte format. While designed to be used together and in the sequence described above, each of the chapter elements can also be employed as freestanding resources.

- You may wish to use the core truth page alone to spark discussion or conversation.

- You can use one of the Bible studies as a personal or group devotional.

- You could assign one of the readings as an advance study assignment for a group, team or class and then process it when you meet together using the application exercise.

Relaxed format. Most people who use the *Essentials* books in a group setting find that the content of each chapter creates more discussion than can be contained in a single group meeting. It is not uncommon for groups to devote two or even three ninety-minute sessions to processing a single chapter. To make best use of the time:

- Be certain that group members do the studies and reading on their own in advance.

- Confine your discussion to no more than three or four questions on each page.

- Focus on the topics and questions that most intrigue or trouble group members.

Focused format—for small group use (90 minutes). A group can get through an entire chapter in one sitting, provided that a disciplined facilitator is designated to focus interaction as follows:

- *Core Truth (whole group—10 minutes):* Ask the group to share key words or phrases that particularly struck them. What was the important insight that spoke to them?

- *Memory Verse (pairs or triads—15 minutes):* Recite the verses to each other and then interact over the inductive questions.

- *Bible Study (whole group—25 minutes):* Capture the highlights of the biblical passage by interacting over the inductive questions.

- *Application Exercise (pairs or triads—30 minutes):* The group leader suggests which of the application questions and/or activities are to be discussed.

- *Closing (whole group—10 minutes):* Come together for any closing remarks and/or invite participants to share where they were personally engaged or stretched by the application exercise.

Focused format—for large group/class use (90 minutes). For a group larger than twelve persons or in a more formal classroom setting, the following format provides room for some active teaching:

- *Introduction (pairs—5 minutes):* The teacher/trainer asks the participants to pair up and share their summary of what the lesson is all about and any truth or insight that was particularly helpful.

- *Core Truth (teacher—5 minutes):* The teacher/trainer highlights key words and phrases, underscoring their importance to the central truth.

- *Memory Verse (pairs—15 minutes):* Paired members recite the verses to each other and then interact over the inductive questions.

- *Bible Study (whole group—5 minutes):* The teacher/trainer uses the inductive guide for group interaction, adding his or her own research and insight to further unpack the text.

- *Application Exercise (pairs or triads—30 minutes):* The teacher/trainer assigns interaction over a few of the application items.

- *Closing (whole group—10 minutes):* The teacher/trainer asks the class members to share any growth steps that they experienced as a result of this lesson. She or he then offers any closing exhortation desired and underlines the assignment for next time.

Focused format—for ministry team use (45 minutes). Ministry teams generally meet at regular intervals (e.g., monthly) and have to balance the spiritual growth dimensions of team life with the ministry tasks to be accomplished. This format is designed for the narrower window of study that these dual demands necessitate.

- *Advance preparation (as needed):* The team leader asks teammates to complete all the parts of the lesson, including the Scripture memory, in advance. State that when you are together, you will pay special attention to the "Application Exercise" section.

- *Whole group discussion (10 minutes):*
  1. How would you summarize what this chapter is all about?
  2. Was there a particular truth, spiritual insight or practical measure that particularly spoke to you?

- *Triad discussion (30 minutes):*
  1. Recite the Scripture Memory verse(s) to one another. What was the value for you of memorizing this particular Scripture?
  2. Discuss the questions in the Application Exercise that seemed most helpful.

- *Whole group closing (5 minutes):* Solicit any insight or action step from the triads that could be beneficial for the whole ministry team to hear.

WHAT ARE THE KEY TERMS USED IN THIS BOOK?

The different ways that various people define key terms (such as *evangelism*) create confusion that inhibits witness. For this reason, I want to lay down some definitions at the outset. You are welcome to challenge my understanding, but you will at least know what I intended to say. Each of the following terms is presented in order of the *breadth* I consider them to encompass—the most embracing to the least.

- *Salvation.* I understand salvation to mean the gracious action of God in Jesus Christ whereby human beings are spared the penalty due upon sin, are made right with God and become full heirs of all his promises through the merit of Christ alone. A major aim of this book is to reclaim the full biblical value of this word. In some circles, salvation has come to be thought of almost solely in terms of justification. While this is its preeminent effect, I understand salvation to embrace also the sanctification, revelation, redemption, resurrection and glorification which God has promised to his heirs. More on this in chapter two.

- *Gospel.* Except when it is used in reference to a particular New Testament book, I take this word to mean the good news of salvation proclaimed by the prophets, angels, Christ and his church through the ages. I will often capitalize this word as a reminder of the larger understanding of salvation stressed above.

- *Discipleship.* This term is used to refer to the life lived in response to the reception of the gospel of salvation and in submission to Christ's lordship.

- *Witness.* I define witness as the process by which someone bears external evidence of discipleship, to the end that God is glorified and others are drawn toward him. While many people equate witness with verbal testimony, in its fullest biblical sense witness or witnessing refers to the message a disciple's *whole life* gives to the transforming power of Jesus Christ.

- *Evangelism*. This term refers to the specific act by which a witness invites someone to receive the gospel of salvation and become a disciple of Jesus Christ.

- *Disciple*. This word identifies someone who is actively walking the pathway of discipleship marked out by Jesus. I will sometimes use the word *Christian* to describe such a person, but I believe that this term has become devalued in our time for reasons that will be described.

- *Nondisciple*. I will use this term as my preferred way of speaking of someone who is not yet a disciple of Jesus. It embraces those who would not call themselves "Christian," but also those who may describe themselves as Christians in a cultural sense but who have not yet accepted the new identity, power and purpose for living that an intentional journey with Jesus entails.

Mnemonic devices. Throughout this book I have made liberal use of acrostics (words whose individual letters signify additional concepts) and alliterations (words beginning with the same consonant) in order to make key concepts and frameworks easier to remember and employ. Translators from the English text will be free to abandon these conventions as faithfulness to their context requires.

CONCLUSION

In the coming pages, we are going to reflect together on the wonderful role that you and I have been called to play as witnesses of Jesus Christ and the gospel of his kingdom. We are going to catch a fresh vision of the staggering influence God wants our lives to have upon the people of this world and how it can happen. As Hudson Taylor, the great missionary to China, once wrote, "God isn't looking for people of great faith, but for individuals ready to follow Him. . . . God uses men [and women] who are weak and feeble enough to lean on him." If you are willing to lean on and learn of Christ, amazing things can happen. Let this be your prayer as we go forward:

> Almighty God, you alone possess the power to draw human hearts to yourself and accomplish the salvation that you have purposed. Humbly leaning upon you and your grace, do in me and through me what you long to do. Use this book to teach me more of your way, to fill me with a greater desire to walk in it, and to bring forth the good for which you have made me your disciple. Through Jesus Christ I pray. Amen.

---

[1]Shared at a gathering of senior pastors at a meeting of Churches United in Global Mission.
[2]Michael L. Simpson, *Permission Evangelism: When to Talk, When to Walk* (Colorado Springs: Cook Communications, 2003), p. 15.

Part One

SEEING THE BIG PICTURE

The job of being a witness can feel overwhelming at the start. Where do I begin? Is there a job description for this? Am I qualified for this work? If you think to ask such questions, it is a sign that you're serious about your role. That is appropriate. After becoming a faithful disciple, the most important question Christians ought to ask is: How do I become a faithful witness? How do I let what God is doing in me move out through me to this world he so loves (John 3:16)?

Before rushing into the "how-to" part, however, it will benefit you greatly to have an understanding of the big picture first. Think of this section as a Newcomer's Orientation to the larger historical, theological and cultural context in which you'll be doing your job. You might not be such a newcomer to the work of witness. Nonetheless, if you can get an even deeper appreciation for the bigger setting, you'll find that the how-to's we'll explore later will make even more sense.

Believe in the Call and Power of God (chap. 1). We're going to start by examining the broad historical context in which you and I do our work as witnesses. We are part of a magnificent movement of God's grace spreading through history. We'll look at Christ's original use of the word *witness* and the compelling charge and promise he associated with it. We'll then see how that commission worked its way out through the centuries. Seeing what God has done in the past and promised for the future will keep us from being discouraged when the work of witness gets challenging in our time.

Examine the News (chap. 2). Next we'll zoom in on the theological and practical content of the message we're seeking to share. Many people have a sadly limited understanding of what the gospel truly is. If we're going to pass it on, it is also essential that you and I see the full meaning of the salvation Christ offers to people. We'll look at the message of Jesus in light of the serious human issues revealed in our everyday news. You'll walk away from that chapter with a much deeper appreciation for just how good the good news truly is.

Mourn the Changed Conditions (chap. 3). We'll close out this section of the book by reviewing some of the massive changes in the cultural context in which disciples in the West seek to share their faith today. As public support for Christians has died out, many Christians have entered into a grieving process that has made it even more difficult to bear witness constructively. Understandable though this is, it is now time to accept this death and move on. The good news is that the present conditions offer us a marvelous opportunity to recover the character of a first-century faith.

With this introduction, then, let's start our study of this bigger picture.

1 / Believe in the Call and Power of God

LOOKING AHEAD

MEMORY VERSE: Acts 1:8
BIBLE STUDY: Hebrews 11:1–12:3
READING: The Spreading Life

 Core Truth

What is the life-changing call and promise that Jesus gives to his disciples?

No less than the first disciples, we are called by Jesus and empowered by his Spirit to play a personally active role in the ultimately unstoppable expansion of Christ's life-redeeming influence, until that coming day when God completes the renewal of his creation. There is no vocation more significant and satisfying than being a witness to the life-changing love of Jesus Christ.

1. Identify key words or phrases in the question and answer above, and state their meaning in your own words.

2. Restate the core truth in your own words.

3. What questions or issues does the core truth raise for you?

Memory Verse Study Guide

Copy the entire text here:

_____

_____

_____

_____

_____

_____

_____

_____

_____

_____

_____

_____

_____

_____

_____

_____

_____

Memory Verse: Acts 1:8

The last words that people speak before leaving loved ones are often very significant. On the last day of his earthly ministry, Jesus issued a specific charge and promise to his disciples concerning the role they would play in his ongoing work in the world. These words are of profound significance for all of us who seek to follow Christ today.

1. *Putting it in context: Read Acts 1:1-11.* What do you imagine the disciples may be thinking and feeling as they stand with Jesus in this scene?

2. According to Acts 1:1-3, what reason would the disciples have for trusting the promise that Jesus makes to them in verse 8?

3. In verses 4-5, Jesus issues a very specific instruction to his disciples. Why was this command and promise important to the work he would ultimately do through them?

4. Jesus tells his disciples that they will be his *witnesses*. When you read that word, what images come to mind?

5. In verse 8, Jesus describes four spheres in which his disciples are to be his witnesses. What are those spheres?

6. What might be the equivalent environments in your life?

7. How have these verses spoken to you?

Inductive Bible Study Guide

Bible Study: Hebrews 11:1–12:3

The book of Hebrews describes the glorious heritage of faithfulness to God and by God in which followers of Jesus stand. This history is instructive to believers in the present as we face the challenges and opportunities of witnessing to Christ in our time.

1. *Read Hebrews 11:1–12:3*. How would you define faith and its importance in light of Hebrews 11:1-2?

2. What are the common characteristics (e.g., circumstances, convictions, conduct) of the faithful people described in chapter 11?

3. *Review Hebrews 11:39-40*. These verses suggest that though they did not experience the fulfillment of all that God had promised, these disciples kept their faith. How easy or hard do you find this kind of faithfulness in your life?

4. *Review Hebrews 12:1-2*. What are the specific instructions we are given in these verses and the realities the writer cites to motivate this behavior?

5. *Review Hebrews 12:3.* What are the two dangers the writer is trying to warn us about as we seek to be like Jesus and the "cloud of witnesses" who have gone before us?

6. As you consider your calling to be a witness in the cause of Christ, what could make you "grow weary" or "lose heart" (Hebrews 12:3)?

7. What questions or issues does this passage raise for you?

DEEP IN OUR HEARTS, WE ALL WANT TO FIND AND FULFILL A PURPOSE BIGGER THAN OURSELVES. ONLY SUCH A LARGER PURPOSE CAN INSPIRE US TO HEIGHTS WE KNOW WE COULD NEVER REACH ON OUR OWN. FOR EACH OF US THE REAL PURPOSE IS PERSONAL AND PASSIONATE: TO KNOW WHAT WE ARE HERE TO DO AND WHY.

Os Guinness

Reading: The Spreading Life

THE SEED OF DEATH?

When it comes to sharing the gospel today, many of us frankly feel somewhat apathetic or insecure. One reason for this deficit is the absence of a clear and accurate picture of the role that the Christian mission and people like us have played in the great sweep of history. Renewing that vision is the aim of this chapter.

This quest for the truth becomes more urgent in light of the particular *version* of history being advanced by a variety of articulate atheists or "anti-theists" today. They assert that a serious study of the past demonstrates that Christianity—along with other religious beliefs—is not benevolent, or merely benign, but actually *bad*. It is antiquated, superstitious and ultimately destructive. It is responsible for incalculable bloodshed, unforgivable injustice and mind-numbing ignorance. Far from being a blessing to human civilization, "faith" has been a blight to human advancement. One of the "new atheists" sums up the conclusion this way: "I can't believe there is a thinking person here who doesn't realize that our species would begin to grow to something like its full height . . . if it emancipated itself from this sinister, childish [religious] nonsense."[1]

Although this opinion is being peddled with fresh packaging today it is hardly new. This view of history first gained prominence back in the late eighteenth century with the widespread reading of Edward Gibbon's book *The History of the Decline and Fall of the Roman Empire.* Gibbon caricatured Christianity as having brought down the grandeur of classical civilization—fettering the human spirit and the life of the mind to which Greece and Rome gave birth. As Christianity expanded, says Gibbon, it weakened the Roman Empire, paving the way for the church to take over and subject the Western world to its superstitions and regressive rules.

As this storyline goes, the church went on to ban books, suppress science and womanhood, and plunge once-noble Europe into the Dark Ages. Bent on taxing people to fund their material and moral excesses, the church's leadership crusaded across the Middle Ages, skewering infidels, racking skeptics and burning dissidents. Thankfully, however, some courageous intellectuals finally revolted against the church's Darth Vader–like grip and birthed the Renaissance. They followed it up with the magnificent Enlightenment, staving back blind religion. In time, thank Man's goodness, these bright thinkers managed to invent the modern era and bring us to the present moment when—if with John Lennon we dare to *imagine*—we can be

> WHERE THERE IS NO VISION, THE PEOPLE PERISH.
>
> Proverbs 29:18 KJV

free of the Christian disease once and for all and enter a new age of progress and peace. In fact, we would have had that better world a whole lot earlier if that Easter hoax had never happened.

This is what is being taught as "history." Can you see why people steeped in this tale might be resistant to the Christian message or discouraged about sharing it with others?

THE ENEMY IS PARTLY RIGHT

As we'll see, however, this storyline is quite a revision of history. Before going there, however, it would serve God's reputation and our credibility well to make the same confession once voiced by Tony Campolo: "We have met the enemy and they are partly right."[2] Jesus once said that only the truth can set us fully free to be his people (John 8:32). The painful truth is that atheism has a foothold today in part because there have been many times in history when

> THE GREATEST CHALLENGE FACING THE CHURCH IN ANY AGE IS THE CREATION OF A LIVING, BREATHING, WITNESSING COLONY OF TRUTH. . . . THE CHALLENGE IS TO ALLOW OURSELVES TO BE SO UTTERLY SHAPED AND FILLED BY THE HOLY CULTURE OF THE KINGDOM OF GOD THAT WHEREVER WE ARE—WHETHER GATHERED TOGETHER IN WORSHIP HERE OR SCATTERED FOR SERVICE ELSEWHERE— WE NEVER LOSE OUR DISTINCTIVENESS. TO MEET ONE OF US IN THE WORKPLACE OR IN THE SCHOOL OR NEIGHBORHOOD OUGHT TO TURN HEADS, AND PROMPT QUESTIONS, AND INSPIRE DESIRE TO KNOW FROM WHAT OTHER NATION WE COME.
>
> Stanley Hauerwas and William Willimon

people of Christian faith (or marching beneath some other religion's flag) have sinned boldly against God and people. Whether by ignorance, pride, greed or some other deadly sin, they have repeated the very atrocities by which ostensibly religious people crucified Jesus because he threatened their institutional power or personal throne.

Over the centuries, Christians have at times been racially, sexually, politically and socially bigoted in ways contrary to the full counsel of Scripture. We have sometimes looked to our own interests more than to the character of Christ or the needs of the world God so loves. We have justified our actions by selective reading of the Bible. If we've grown up believing that the Christian church or our Christian nation or anything other than Christ himself is substantially holier than everyone else, then the attacks of contemporary atheists are actually God's good gift. They invite us to re-call that we too need the Savior and that he is not done renovating our lives.

At the same time, if we allow the anti-theist's rewriting of history to stand un-challenged, we will sacrifice truth, im-peril the future and cripple our ability to present the evangelistic witness still so needed in our day. To paraphrase Max DePree's famous maxim about leadership: "The first responsibility of a *witness* is to *define reality*."[3] Here, then, is the larger reality that is the true context for our witness and the greater story into which God is drawing you.

THE PANDO PATTERN

High in the Wasatch Mountains of Utah stands a magnificent aspen forest. If you could visit that place today, you would be amazed by the beauty and abundance of life beneath that golden canopy. What would be less obvious is that what appears to the eye as a massive forest is, in reality, just one tree. That's right: *one* tree. At the center of that forest stands a particu-larly ancient tree that researchers have dubbed "Pando"—a Latin word meaning "I spread." Over the ages, Pando spread out its roots across a span of more than 100 acres. It sent up more than 47,000 in-dividual offshoots. Each of these shoots became a new spire reaching toward the heavens, a new crown of leaves moving to the wind, a new sanctuary for the crea-tures who find life beneath Pando's shel-tering arms. Many regard Pando as the world's most massive living entity.[4]

But that honor truly belongs to Another.

Following his crucifixion, the body of Jesus was taken down from the cross, pre-pared for burial and laid in a tomb like a seed in the ground (Luke 23:50-56). Fear-ing that his disciples might try to steal the corpse and propagate the myth of his resur-rection, the local religious leaders went to the Roman governor, Pilate, and convinced him to secure the grave. Pilate ordered the tomb sealed and an armed detail posted at the entrance to guard against any possible invasion (Matthew 27:62-66). What no human authority anticipated, however, was that the source of invasion would not be from outside the tomb but from within it. As Jesus had promised, his seed had fallen to the ground and died. It was now about to rise up again and spread out into the world with a power and productivity no human eye could yet see (John 12:23-34).

On Easter morning, the disciples went to the tomb and found the guards gone, the stone rolled away and the corpse of Jesus missing. The grave clothes in which they'd wrapped his body now lay on the ground like an empty seed casing. To their utter shock, they met the "dead" man, now clearly alive in a way that recast forever their un-derstanding of Life and proved the reliability of all that Jesus had taught them (Luke 24).

Over the next forty days, Jesus appeared to his followers at many times and places, in a manner that seemed designed to dem-onstrate conclusively that this was no hal-lucination (1 Corinthians 15:1-8). Jesus continued to teach his disciples about the kingdom that God sought to bring forth on the earth (Acts 1:3). Finally, Jesus told them that it was time for him to leave them, but gave the assurance that they would not be left alone. Christ promised to send his Holy Spirit to them and that this Spirit would supply them with all they needed to accomplish the next stage of God's purposes in history. "Do not leave Jerusalem," he said, "but wait for the gift my Father promised" (Acts 1:4).

The disciples were filled (as we often are) with misgivings (Acts 1:6). They saw a world in need of such dramatic change and could not imagine how the work of Christ could go on without him walking next to them. But Jesus clarified his plan even further. He said, "You will receive power when the Holy Spirit comes on you; and you will be my witnesses in Jerusalem, and in all Judea and Samaria, and to the ends of the earth" (Acts 1:8). *You* will become the body through which I now live on earth. *You* will be the ones through whom I draw the world to myself. I will supply *you* with the *power* to accomplish my purposes.

This promise was every bit as outrageous as the original assertion that he would rise from the grave. But given the fulfillment of the first promise, the disciples dared to trust the second. They obeyed Christ's command to stay in Jerusalem, though they risked arrest. They waited "all together in one place" (Acts 2:1).

And then, very suddenly, the Power came. "Like the blowing of a violent wind," like "tongues of fire that separated and came to rest on each of them," the Holy Spirit of God filled the house and, more

important, their hearts, so that they began to proclaim the message of the kingdom of God (Acts 2:2-4). Bursting out from the building they'd been hiding in, those first disciples became an unstoppable force of boldness and blessing. As Acts goes on to record, they became a wave of witnesses through whom God began to turn the Roman world upside down (Acts 17:6).

THE LIFE OF CHRIST SPREADS

In his book *The Rise of Christianity*,[5] Rodney Stark reports that at the time of Christ's death (c. A.D. 30) there were only a handful of believers, hardly enough to constitute a single church. Thirty years later, there were still only an estimated 3,000 converts, a handful of struggling churches, and mounting opposition and violence from the surrounding culture. Sociologists of religion tell us that it is at this sort of juncture that new spiritual movements typically face the brutal fact that the forces against them are too great. They surrender their efforts to expand, turn inward and begin to die. That is why what actually happened next has forced more than a few skeptics to conclude that Christianity had its roots in something (or Someone) substantially different than other movements.

Rodney Stark found that between A.D. 60 and 100, the number of Christians suddenly more than doubled to 7,500, and then exploded to more than 40,000 people by the year 150. By A.D. 200, the total number of Christ-followers exceeded 200,000. It quintupled to one million by 250 and then rocketed to a staggering six million by the turn of 300. Over the next fifty years, the church more than quintupled again, producing some 33 million confessing Christians—half the citizenry of the Roman Empire. Over the coming centuries, the church of Jesus would continue to spread out till its branches defined the character of what we now call Western civilization.

The phenomenal growth of Christianity's tree prompts the question *Why?* Rodney Stark writes: "How did a tiny and obscure messianic movement from the edge of the Roman Empire dislodge classical paganism and become the dominant faith of Western Civilization?"[6] The answer is an essential one for anyone interested in being part of the continuing movement of the gospel today. It is a very different story from the one you or the people you seek to reach may have been told.

RECLAIMING HISTORY

As the witnesses of Jesus began to spread out from Jerusalem in the middle of the first century, Roman civilization was already on the rocks. It was nothing like the Golden Society that Edward Gibbon so romantically pictures. Roman culture was morally wasting, ravaged by political divisions and scandalized by widespread slavery, the commonly accepted abuse of children, and a widening gap between the haves and the never-would-haves. When the Huns, Goths and other northern tribes finally poured down into the heart of Europe they found a society so soft and rotting that they sliced through it like a laser through an overripe tomato. It was not the church

but Roman decadence and barbarian pillaging which created the Dark Ages.

People today are routinely taught that it was the support of the Roman Empire under Constantine that led to the explosive growth of Christianity. In reality, however, it was the *collapse* of that Empire that unleashed the church to play the strategic role God had for it in this part of history. As Dinesh D'Souza observes, "Slowly and surely, Christianity took this backward continent and gave it learning and order, stability and dignity."[7] Bit by bit, the distinctive beliefs and practices of Christ's followers began the profound reshaping of Western civilization.

Learning and literature. Because Christians believed that Christ was Lord of all the earth and that God had left the stamp of his eternal nature in the heart of all people (Ecclesiastes 3:11), Christian monks highly valued what was left of classical civilization, particularly its arts and letters. As Thomas Cahill has documented well, the monks studied, copied and hid away the manuscripts that preserved the learning of late antiquity—saving for us the remaining treasures of Greece and Rome.[8]

Commerce and capitalism. Because Christian theology held that God was the divine Logos (John 1:1-5)—the great mind that brought intelligent structure and order out of chaos—Christian monasteries became radiant centers of organized community and personal industry throughout Europe. They applied biblical principles of private property, civic stewardship and limited government to a world that had largely lost these values. Out of the wasteland of the Dark Ages, Christians produced hamlets, towns and eventually cities. The principles of commerce and elected leadership practiced in those monastic communities created the foundation for capitalism and democratic society as we know them today.

Dignity and charity. Steadily, the Christian missionary movement stretched out, converting the Northern European barbarian hordes, the Angles and Saxons, and the tribes of Scotland, Ireland and Wales. Warriors gradually became knights, infused now with new ideals of civility and chivalry that still inform our society. Because Jesus honored women and valued children, the developing civilization of Europe began to take on his imprint in these ways, albeit imperfectly, but to an extent utterly foreign to other cultures of that time and to many in ours today. Because Jesus had said: "Whatever you do for one of the least—the poor, the imprisoned, the sick—you do for me" (Matthew 25:31-46, my paraphrase), Christ's followers showed concern for the weak and the marginalized. They developed innumerable hospitals, orphanages and other centers of charity, again, to an extent unknown before on planet Earth.

Science and higher education. Other religions, including the classic Greek and Roman ones, held that the gods (and therefore the movements of nature) were capricious or unknowable. But Christians believed that God was rational and had given human beings minds to discover his glory in the created order. Episodes of regression aside, Christianity was indisputably the world's most massive sponsor of the scientific enterprise and the academic culture that fostered it. The Christian passion for the pursuit of truth led to the establishment of an untold number of schools and universities. Go study the inscriptions carved into the stones of the Western world's greatest institutions of higher education and you will be thunderstruck by the prevalence of the biblical imprint there.

The modern world. Yale professor Jaroslav Pelikan remarks that

> Jesus of Nazareth has been the dominant figure in the history of Western culture for almost twenty centuries. If it were possible, with some sort of

> IT IS IN THE VERY BEING OF GOD THAT THE BASIS FOR THE MISSIONARY ENTERPRISE IS FOUND. GOD IS A SENDING GOD, WITH A DESIRE TO SEE HUMANKIND AND CREATION RECONCILED, REDEEMED, AND HEALED. THE MISSIONAL CHURCH, THEN, IS A SENT CHURCH. IT IS A GOING CHURCH, A MOVEMENT OF GOD THROUGH HIS PEOPLE, SENT TO BRING HEALING TO A BROKEN WORLD.
>
> Michael Frost and Alan Hirsch

super magnet, to pull up out of that history every scrap of metal bearing at least a trace of His name, how much would be left?[9]

In his book *The Victory of Reason,* Stark answers that question:

> Had the followers of Jesus remained an obscure Jewish sect, most of you would not have learned to read and the rest of you would be reading from hand-copied scrolls. Without a theology committed to reason, progress, and moral equality, today the entire world would be about where non-European societies were in 1800.

It would be, Stark says,

> a world with many astrologers and alchemists but no scientists . . . a world of despots, lacking universities, banks, factories, eyeglasses, chimneys, and pianos . . . a world where most infants do not live to the age of five and many women die in childbirth. The modern world arose only in Christian societies. Not in Islam. Not in Asia. Not in a "secular" society.[10]

There would be no world as we know it today if Easter had never happened.

What Is God Doing Today?

As the writer of Hebrews asserted, Christ calls his witnesses to present God's message of hope despite all opposition (Hebrews 12:3). Today we face an articulate and assertive army of anti-theists who are deeply embedded in our academic institutions and who trumpet their worldview even through the organs of entertainment. They declare that if we could just leave religion behind and build instead on the innate genius and goodness of humanity, we would have a better world.

That "noble experiment," however, has already been tried. It was conducted with great intentionality in Russia, China and Korea during the twentieth century and led to the starvation, slaughter and suppression of millions of lives. Yet people in those same parts of the world are now flocking into house churches, refurbished cathedrals, corporate offices and storefront worship centers by the tens of millions, passionately seeking the generative seed of the Christian gospel.

After nearly a century of state-sponsored atheism in Russia, 74 percent of the population now self-identifies as Christian.[11] In 1900, Korea had no Protestant church and was ruled "impossible to penetrate" by mission organizations. Today, there are 7,000 churches in the city of Seoul alone, one of them numbering 750,000 members.[12] At the turn of the nineteenth century, the southern portion of the African continent was only 3 percent Christian. Today, 63 percent of the population is, while membership in the churches of Africa is increasing by 34,000 new members every day.[13]

In Hindu India, 14 million of the 140 million members of the "untouchable" caste have become Christians.[14] More people in the Islamic world have come to Christ in the last twenty-five years than in the entire history of Christian missions combined.[15] In Islamic Indonesia, the percentage of Christians is now so high (somewhere around 15 percent) and the number of megachurches is growing so quickly that the Muslim government will no longer print the statistics.[16] Back in 1950, there were only a handful of evangelical Christians in Brazil. Today, more than one-fifth of the population self-identifies as Protestant. The Catholic Church in Brazil has experienced a profound revival too, going from 50 million adherents in 1950 to more than 134 million today.[17]

All the talk these days is of the coming influence of China. Yet, as two writers from the *Economist* recently asserted, there are now more self-avowed disciples of Jesus in China than members of the Communist party.[18] David Aikman of the *New York Times* points out that every year there are ten million more converts to Christianity. Even the most conservative estimates suggest that China will soon become the largest Christian country in the world.[19]

Much is also made of the global expansion of Islam, but Christianity—not Islam—is the fastest-spreading faith on earth. By 2050, there will be three Christians for every two Muslims worldwide.[20] Across the planet, followers of Jesus are increasing by more than eighty thousand disciples a day. Five hundred and ten new congregations of Christian worshipers form every day, which is 3,750 every week.[21] The irony is that, except for the Middle East (where it was born) and Europe and America (to whose civilization it gave birth), Christianity is expanding everywhere today (see John 4:44). To put it simply, the gospel of Jesus is going out and growing up in Pando-like proportions.

JOIN IN THE SPREAD

It is essential to remember all this as we begin to think afresh about our work as witnesses today. Without this larger perspective, it is easy for those of us who live in places where the gospel message is not apparently prospering to think that the human heart is just too hard and the heat of opposition just too blazing for the work of Christian witness to succeed in our times. We can be tempted to withdraw into a private piety and give up the dream of life-changing influence on others. But God has not given up his plan to extend his kingdom in the community where you live (Jerusalem), the region where you work (Judea), the areas you try to avoid (Samaria), and to the very ends of the earth (Acts 1:8). As John Piper remarks,

> God is pursuing with omnipotent passion a worldwide purpose of gathering joyful worshipers for Himself from every tribe and tongue and people and nation. He has an inexhaustible enthusiasm for the supremacy of His name among the nations. Therefore, let us bring our affections into line with His, and, for the sake of His name, let us . . . join His global purpose.[22]

It isn't just the job of paid pastors, evangelists and missionaries to scatter the seed of the new life God desires to give to every human being. None other than Jesus himself calls you to take your place among the "great cloud of witnesses" (Hebrews 12:1) through whom he has been spreading his kingdom's life for many centuries and continues to work now throughout our world. You are not a beleaguered minority up against impossible forces. You are a privileged member of the greatest movement in history and the only one that will be around in the end (Revelation 22). Christ has promised to supply you with the power to do this work and, as history shows, Jesus always keeps his promises—even the most outrageous ones.

So, fix your eyes on Jesus, the author and perfecter of our faith. Keep considering him so you don't lose heart. Run with perseverance the good race marked out for you (Hebrews 12:2-3). Let's go forward on this journey together by examining next the content of the message we seek to sow and learning why it is such very good news.

---

[1]Comment made by Christopher Hitchens (author of *God Is Not Great*) at a debate with Alister E. McGrath (author of *The Twilight of Atheism*) at Georgetown University.

[2]Tony Campolo, *Partly Right: Learning from the Critics of Christianity* (Nashville: W Publishing, 1988).

[3]Max DePree, *Leadership Is an Art* (New York: Dell Publishing, 1989).

[4]Michael C. Grant, "The Trembling Giant," *DISCOVER Magazine,* October 1993, discovermagazine.com/1993/oct/thetremblinggian285.

[5]Rodney Stark, *The Rise of Christianity: A Sociologist Reconsiders History* (Princeton, NJ: Princeton University Press, 1996), pp. 4-13.

[6]Ibid., p. 3.

[7]Dinesh D'Souza, *What's So Great About Christianity* (Washington, DC: Regnery, 2007), p. 43.

[8]Thomas Cahill, *How the Irish Saved Civilization* (New York: Anchor Books, 1995), pp. 181-96.

[9]Jaroslav Pelikan, *Jesus Through the Centuries: His Place in the History of Culture* (New Haven, CT: Yale University Press, 1985), p. 1.

[10]Rodney Stark, *The Victory of Reason: How Christianity Led to Freedom, Capitalism and Western Success* (New York: Random House, 2005), p. 233.

[11]Pew Forum on Religion & Public Life, "Global Christianity," December 2011, p. 11.

[12]Dr. H. Vinson Synan, "The Yoido Full Gospel Church," *Cyberjournal for Pentecostal-Charismatic Research,* www.pctii.org/cyberj/cyberj2/synan.html.

[13]"Status of Global Mission, 2011, in Context of 20th and 21st Centuries," January 2011, www.gordonconwell.edu/resources/documents/StatusOfGlobalMission.pdf.

[14]"Number of Christians in China and India," Lausanne Global Analysis, August 7, 2011, *Lausanne Global Conversation,* http://conversation.lausanne.org/en/conversations/detail/11971#article_page_4.

[15]Richard Love, "Discipling All Muslim Peoples in the Twenty-First Century," *International Journal of Frontier Missions* 17, no. 4 (2000), accessed at www.strategicnetwork.org/index.php?loc=kb&view=v&id=18855&printerfriendly=Y&lang=.

[16]Hannah Beech, "Christianity's Surge in Indonesia," *Time,* April 26, 2010, www.time.com/time/magazine/article/0,9171,1982223-1,00.html.

[17]"Global Christianity," December 19, 2011, Pew Forum on Religion & Public Life, http://pewforum.org/Christian/Global-Christianity-brazil.aspx.

[18]John Micklethwait and Adrian Wooldridge, *God Is Back: How the Global Revival of Faith Is Changing the World* (New York: Penguin, 2009), p. 4.

[19]David Aikman, *Jesus in Beijing: How Christianity Is Transforming China and Changing the Global Balance of Power* (Washington, DC: Regnery, 2004).

[20]Peter Jenkins, *The Next Christendom: The Coming of Global Christianity* (London: Oxford University Press, 2002), p. 5.

[21]"Status of Global Mission, 2011."

[22]John Piper, *Let the Nations Be Glad: The Supremacy of God in Missions* (Grand Rapids: Baker Books, 2005), p. 62.

Application Exercise

1. In what ways has the spread of the Christian movement been like the expansion of the aspen forest described in the opening paragraph of the reading?

2. What blessings has the extension of God's kingdom through his witnesses brought about on this earth? List several that particularly impress or encourage you.

3. Of the various criticisms of Christianity leveled by opponents, which ones seem fairest and how do you respond to them?

4. As you think about Christ's call to be his witness and his promise to supply you with the power to do it, what feelings or thoughts does this occasion for you?

5. Does the reading convict, challenge or comfort you? Why?

Going Deeper

D'Souza, Dinesh. *What's So Great About Christianity.* Washington, DC: Regnery, 2007.

2 / Examine the News

LOOKING AHEAD

MEMORY VERSE: Romans 1:16
BIBLE STUDY: Romans 3:9-23; 5:8; 6:23; 10:9-15
READING: The Message in Two Hands

 Core Truth

What is the gospel to which we are called to bear witness?

We are called to proclaim the good news of Christ's life-giving victory over the sinful separation from God that disfigures human character, blinds people to truth and leaves them without reliable power to overcome the brokenness of creation, the darkness of death, and the limits of human love. This gospel is God's wonderful invitation to be saved from sin for a beautiful new life through him.

1. Identify key words or phrases in the question and answer above, and state their meaning in your own words.

2. Restate the core truth in your own words.

3. What questions or issues does the core truth raise for you?

Memory Verse Study Guide

Copy the entire text here:

_____

_____

_____

_____

_____

_____

_____

_____

_____

_____

_____

_____

_____

_____

_____

_____

_____

Memory Verse: Romans 1:16

Gospel is a term whose full meaning is often not grasped, even by those who have been around a church for a very long time. In this study we start to lay a foundation for a fuller understanding of this wonderful message.

1. *Putting it in context:* In his letter to the Romans, the apostle Paul lays out the great doctrines of the Christian faith, introducing us to some significant theological words. What is your best brief definition of each of these?

   a. Justification:

   b. Sanctification:

   c. Revelation:

   d. Redemption:

   e. Resurrection:

   f. Glorification:

2. What do you think Paul meant when he said, "I am not ashamed of the gospel"?

3. Do you ever feel anxious or uncertain about sharing the gospel with others? Why?

4. Paul declares that the gospel is "the power of God for the salvation of everyone who believes." How do you define the word *salvation?*

5. How does salvation relate to those theological words in question 1?

6. How have these verses spoken to you?

Inductive Bible Study Guide

Bible Study: Romans 3:9-23; 5:8; 6:23; 10:9-15

As we'll explore in the reading, the message of salvation addresses many of the crucial issues of human life. Before the gospel can exert its full influence, however, it must meet people at the point of their most fundamental need—their broken relationship with God. In what has come to be known as "the Roman Road to Salvation," the apostle Paul defines this need and its remedy.

1. *Read Romans 3:9-23*, paying especially close attention to verses 10-18 and verse 23. Does this assessment of people and God seem overly pessimistic, realistic or optimistic to you and why?

2. *Read Romans 6:23*. In the first half of the verse, Paul gives his readers some hard news. What does Paul mean by "wages" and "death" here and why is this bad news?

3. In the second half of the verse, Paul shares some fabulously good news. What words are used to describe the good that is offered here and from whence does this good come?

4. *Read Romans 5:8*. What did God demonstrate and why was this necessary?

5. *Read Romans 10:9-13*. Who can be saved and how?

6. What do you think Paul means when he says that "it is with your heart that you believe and are justified" (Romans 10:10), and why is it important that belief be from there and not just with the mind?

7. *Read Romans 10:14-15*. What are the key messages in these verses?

8. What questions or issues do these passages raise for you?

WE ARE HEIR TO A MENTALITY THAT IS BASICALLY DEFENSIVE. WE HAVE RETREATED TO OUR FORTRESSES WITH A DISABLING, DEEP-SEATED INFERIORITY COMPLEX. SUBTLY THE MESSAGE HAS COME THROUGH THAT THE WORLD OUT THERE IS MODERN WHILE WE ARE OLD-FASHIONED. THE WORLD IS SEEN AS MOVING TOO QUICKLY; IT'S TOO AFFLUENT, TOO EDUCATED, TOO SOPHISTICATED TO BE INTERESTED IN BIBLICAL CHRISTIANITY. IN EFFECT, WE ARE ASHAMED OF THE GOSPEL OF JESUS CHRIST. WE DO NOT BELIEVE THAT THE WORLD COULD POSSIBLY WANT WHAT WE HAVE.

Frank Tillapaugh

Reading: The Message in Two Hands

GETTING THE GOSPEL

Jesus has both called and empowered us to take our place among the great cloud of witnesses God is using to advance his redemptive purposes in history. The question that naturally arises is *How?* How do we go about being these witnesses of whom Jesus speaks? The *short* answer to this question is, "by proclaiming the gospel message."

The word *gospel* derives from an old Anglo-Saxon word that means "good message" or "good news." The Bible tells us that "Jesus went about all the cities and villages, teaching in their synagogues, and proclaiming the good news of the kingdom" (Matthew 9:35 NRSV). When giving instructions to his disciples about the role that they were to play, Jesus said, "Go into all the world and proclaim the good news to the whole creation" (Mark 16:15 NRSV). What, then, is this "good news" that we are meant to proclaim?

German theologian Karl Barth once suggested that answering this question requires having a handle on two primary resources. Barth told a group of students that if they wanted to have a significant impact on others, they should take a newspaper in one hand and a Bible in the other, and then help people interpret the former in light of the latter.[1] In other words, to be effective witnesses we need to have a good grasp of both the "daily news" and the "divine news."

THE DAILY NEWS

The news on most days contains plenty of stories about good things happening. There are reports of technological innovations and medical breakthroughs. There are accounts of creative artists and courageous leaders. There are sports scores that make us cheer and tidings of happy events that make us smile. On some days, all seems right with this world. We appear to be addressing our problems, making progress as a people and shaping a planet we can pass on with pride. And then there are those times when it *doesn't* feel that way at all. There are moments when all the positive press does not make up for the persistent *issues* that define too much of this life.

The core issue. Every day we meet people who, for all of their strengths, seem to be operating from a fundamental lack within. Even the most talented or celebrated people still often exhibit a level of grasping, preening and positioning that betrays an emptiness at their core. Many pursue achievements, accolades or acquisitions with an almost desperate anxiety, unable to rest or say "enough." Others jump from one relationship or place to the next, seemingly unable to find a sense of home. Still others are so haunted by their failures or physical imperfections that they seek solace in relentless rounds of alcohol, pills or cosmetic resurfacing. Mark Twain once said that there come these moments when you realize that "you don't quite know what it is you *do* want, but it makes your heart ache, you want it so!"[2] What is this central source of identity or security that seems to be missing in so many people's lives?

The character issue. Without a healthy center, people become unhealthy in all kinds of ways that exact a severe toll on others. We open the morning news only to hear another report about a parent, teacher, coach or religious figure who violated a sacred trust at a terrible cost. We groan at the story of the corporate or political leaders who abused their position so that others now pay. We see excess and vanity routinely paraded as the right of celebrity. We encounter people who eat too often, work too little or demand too much. We learn of another partnership dissolving, another scandal brewing, another act of violence done. Somehow, all of our advances in education, technology and prosperity have not corrected the character issue at the heart

of so much bad news. Is there a solution to this?

The truth issue. Complicating the matter further, there is great disagreement today over whether there exist any objective, dependable spiritual truths that might guide us out of our morass. Many speak as though all religious viewpoints were equal and all ethics relative. This is strange. We would never knowingly board an airplane piloted by someone who did not believe in the law of gravity. We would never submit to the scalpel of a surgeon who believed that the knee bone would work just fine if connected to the collarbone. In almost every dimension of life that matters, we believe that there are certain discernible principles, critical arrangements and proven pathways by which life functions best. Still, many doubt there exists the same kind of dependable framework in the arena or relationship with God, others and self. Is there anywhere a source of purpose or a set of

> IT IS AS THOUGH WE ARE CONTAINERS INTO WHICH WE KEEP POURING THINGS, BUT WE NEVER GET FILLED UP BECAUSE THERE IS A HOLE IN EACH CONTAINER AND SOMETHING IS ALWAYS LEAKING OUT. SO WE SPEND OUR LIVES TRYING TO ATTAIN FULLNESS, SATISFACTION, AND COMPLETENESS, AND YET WE NEVER DO. WE GO ON THINKING THAT IF ONLY WE HAD JUST A BIT MORE, THEN WE WOULD BE SATISFIED; IF WE HAD SOMETHING ELSE, THEN OUR POTENTIAL WOULD BE REALIZED, OUR HAPPINESS ASSURED, AND OUR FULFILLMENT ACHIEVED.
> Diogenes Allen

principles for human living that can be demonstrated to have produced a way of life healthier for the broadest range of people than all the others in the marketplace of ideas?

The change issue. The news today is also colored by problems that seem intractable. In our inner cities, school systems are often under-resourced and educational outcomes atrocious. A stunningly high percentage of homes are parented by single moms or the gangs that have taken in largely fatherless children. Desperate teens are locked into a cycle of crime and incarceration. Across the world, millions of children die of malnutrition and disease for which solutions exist, while millions more are aborted or abandoned. A scandalous number of the elderly and the mentally ill languish without people to visit them. We who are affluent often expend staggering resources to buy products we do not need with money we do not have to impress people we do not particularly like. The landfills expand while the rainforests shrink. Governments remain gridlocked by special interests while citizens feel helpless or distracted by their own interests. Where will we find the perspective and power to change these conditions?

The mortality issue. As if all these issues were not dark enough, lingering over human life is the ultimate shadow. Sooner or later, the people with whom we've laughed and learned will wither away and be seen no more on this earth. Each year, illness and accident snuff out the flame of precious people who seemed to have so much more living to do. The obituary pages of our newspapers are crammed with microprint, vainly trying to tell the stories of individuals whose actual imprint on others was so large the entire paper wouldn't be sufficient to do justice to the story. And one day it will be your name there, or mine, on a tombstone someplace, sidled up next to two dates, an entire lifetime reduced to an intervening dash. Is this all there is?

The love issue. It would be bearable, perhaps, to think that this life is all there is if the journey here were largely filled with love. If each of us went through our days surrounded by people who loved us with a pure and unwavering consistency, or if we were able to love others with a steady, unfettered compassion, this life might well seem enough. At the end of the day, love is what matters most. Yet, in the stories of children forgotten or used, in the tales of marriages or business relationships torn asunder, in the record of politicians and pundits shredding others without civility, we see the face of a world where love is too little. How could it become otherwise?

Summing it up. As stated earlier, there are always positive reports, entertainments and distractions to keep us from despair about all this. But denial or diversion is not what people need today. As Karl Barth saw clearly, what is needed most are people who know how to interpret the daily news in the light and power of a far greater message. This is the job of Christ's witnesses.

THE STORY BEHIND THE NEWS

The Bible teaches that behind all the news of today lies a larger storyline which not only explains our present predicament but also pictures our way out of it. The major elements of this "salvation history" (as theologians have called it) are worth our review.

Creation. The Scriptures say that, "in the beginning, God" occupied a place as the generative center of his creation. He was recognized by human beings as the source of all light, love and life. Because of him and our relationship with him, we truly had it all. We had an unimpeachable identity as children of the Creator himself. We walked "naked and unashamed" with one another. We had a clear purpose for our lives as stewards of his creation. We had eternal life, because *his* life moved through us. There was no anxiety or fear, no hiding or hurting, no sense of toil about our days. It was just life *with* God and *for* God and *in* God, and "it was very good" (Genesis 1).

Fall. And then, moved by an impulse so blind and counterproductive that theologians have called it "the mystery of iniquity" or "original sin," human beings decided that this very good life was not good enough. Seduced into thinking we would be better off assuming the god-role ourselves, we willfully broke our bond of relationship with God. We denied our dependence upon him. We appropriated the authority to define good and evil ourselves. Instead of gaining us the greater paradise that grasping pride promised us, our choice won us only an increasingly bleak wilderness. Instead of rising, we fell (Genesis 2–3).

Immediate consequences. The choice to banish God from the center of human life had a cascade of consequences, vividly evidenced in the next chapters of Genesis, in the history of Israel, and in the news today. It brought division and destruction between people because, without the Source of *love,* human differences and imperfections inevitably divide and destroy us. It brought darkness and despair into human life because, without the Source of *light,* we don't see truth or why stuffing into the hole at our center everything but the One who is needed to fill it cannot satisfy us. It brought decay and death into the world because without the Source of *life* there is only the inevitable march toward the entropy and eradication of all we hold dear. But there are even worse consequences.

Eternal consequences. The Bible declares that the ultimate outcome of our choice to be our own god is that we risk being without the real God forever. We become like an astronaut who has repeatedly been invited to come back into the spaceship, yet whose lifeline has finally broken under the strain of his repeated pushing away. Now he drifts forever in a place of unbearable coldness and isolation, left to his own resources alone. Jesus used equally vivid images in an effort to make the reality of hell clear to people of his day. Far from being the cosmic Las Vegas people joke about, Jesus likened it to a trash heap, a lake of fire, an outer darkness, a place of weeping and gnashing of teeth. Do everything you can to keep yourself and those you know from this destination, says Jesus, for if one dies without being reunited with God the separation will be permanent (Matthew 5:29-30; 25:30; Revelation 19:20).

Amazing grace. Having seen us spurn his offer of relationship in favor of life on our terms, God would be well within his rights to wash his hands of the human race and leave us with our "issues" for all eternity. But here is where we meet the only wonder larger than that of human iniquity—the mystery of divine grace.

- *He came to us.* Seeking to save his creatures from the consequences of their sin, God crossed the vast gulf between us. He became a hungry child to an impoverished family in a war-ravaged land. Stretching out to us his *two seeking hands*, God said, in effect: "I know how hard this life has become. I've come to share it with you and to remind you that it was not meant to be this way. It can be different."

- *He gave his life for us.* Substituting himself in the place of judgment that our depravity deserved, Jesus became the one sacrifice worthy enough to cancel out the weight of human sin, balancing the scales of justice with mercy. Upon the cross, Jesus stretched out to us his *two nail-pierced hands*, saying, "I know the horror of what sin does and deserves, but I am taking it all upon myself here so you can go free."

- *He offered new life to us.* And then, rising from the grave to prove he has

the power to fulfill his promises, God stretched out to us his *two sovereign hands.* "Come home," he says. "All is forgiven. Be my children again. I will be the light, the love, the life at your center" (Luke 15; John 1:1-14, my paraphrase).

THE DIVINE NEWS

In a nutshell, this is the divine news we call the gospel. "For God so loved the world that he gave his one and only Son, that whoever believes in him shall not perish but have eternal life. For God did not send his Son into the world to condemn the world, but to save the world through him" (John 3:16-17).

There are many ways of describing the salvation that God offers us in Christ, as we'll learn when we reach chapter eleven in this book. There are also several dimensions to this salvation. Only by considering them can we see just *how good* the divine news truly is.

1. You can get right with God (justification). The most important idea for Christ's witnesses to pass on to others is that there is an answer to the *core issue* of human life. "For God was in Christ," writes Paul, "reconciling the world to himself, no longer counting people's sins against them. And he gave us this wonderful message of reconciliation" (2 Corinthians 5:19 NLT). Our ultimate aim as witnesses is to help people see that any of us can begin our relationship with God anew. All you need do is:

- *Acknowledge* that you have been living

separated from God because of your desire to be your own god and that this way leads to judgment and death (Romans 3:23; 6:23).

- *Believe* that Jesus' sacrifice on the cross proves that God's love for you is larger than your sin and provides the payment that spares you from judgment (Romans 5:8-11; 6:23).

- *Confess* your need of God's mercy and grace at the core of your life and ask him to come take up permanent residence there (Romans 10:9-13; Revelation 3:20).

- *Dedicate* yourself to following Jesus for life (John 10:27-29). Resolve that he will not only be your Savior, but also your Lord.

This wonderful message is the core of the gospel. The theological word for it is "justification," and it simply means that we can "get right" with God. In its fullest sense, however, the gospel is about much more than this. Salvation is not only about establishing a new relationship *with* God; it is also about experiencing a new life *through* God. Christ doesn't just save us *from* sin; he saves us *for* a glorious new kind of life (1 Peter 2:9-12). Let's look together at some of these further dimensions of the gospel message.

2. You can overcome your character flaws (sanctification). The good news is that once we have welcomed God into our core, he can begin to address the character issue that previously limited us. Jesus said, "I have come that [you] may have life, and

. . . have it more abundantly" (John 10:10 NKJV). He also promised that "If you remain in me and I in you, you will bear much fruit" (John 15:5). Jesus was saying that as his Spirit fills us from the center, he will grow in us a "love, joy, peace, patience, kindness, goodness, faithfulness, gentleness and self-control" like his. The apostle Paul called these Christlike character traits "the fruit of the Spirit" (Galatians 5:22-23). The theological word for this process of transformation of character is *sanctification* (literally, being "made holy"). As my friend Greg Ogden remarks, the good news we can share with others is that in Christ their very best selves await them.

3. You can set your course by reliable truth (revelation). A further element of the gospel is that we no longer need to live in confusion when it comes to the *truth issue*. Jesus said, "I am the way and the truth and the life" and "If you hold to my teaching, you are really my disciples. . . . You will know the truth, and the truth will set you free" (John 14:6; 8:31). In other words, Christ's witnesses proclaim the good news that there are, in fact, absolutely reliable principles on which we can set our course and build a healthier life. Jesus and his disciples can teach them to us (Matthew 11:26-27; 28:18-20). Jesus also promised that when the Holy Spirit comes into the life of a disciple "he will guide you into all truth" (John 16:13).

This process of Spirit-empowered guidance goes by the theological word *revelation*. Christian discipleship involves learning to live our whole lives in response to the truth that the Holy Spirit impresses upon us. The Spirit speaks truth directly into the minds of Christ's disciples, but he will never say anything contrary to what he has already revealed in God's Word. In the Bible we find practical truth about how to overcome temptation, resolve conflicts, communicate with others, manage money, raise children, lead people and live wisely and well in scores of other spheres of life (2 Timothy 3:16-17). In a world that is struggling for direction in all of these areas, this is very good news indeed.

4. You can participate in the renewal of this world (redemption). The gospel message is also good news for everyone concerned about the *change issue* explored earlier in this reading. On the day that Christ ascended into heaven, the first disciples were filled with a similar concern. They saw their nation still overrun by a cruel power and beset with so many intractable problems (Acts 1:6). But the angels that spoke to them that day reminded them that this Jesus they'd seen go into heaven was going to come back one day (Acts 1:11). When he comes the second time, the Bible declares, Christ will make everything new. "There will be no more death or mourning or crying or pain, for the old order of things [will have] passed away" (Revelation 21:5).

The theological word for this renewal of the whole creation is "redemption." It comes from a word used in the slave markets of ancient times to refer to the act of "buying back" or "purchasing the freedom of" a slave *(apolutroseos)*. On the cross,

Jesus paid the price required to buy his world back from its bondage to sin and death. He now plans to restore not just individuals but the whole of his creation to its intended state. If you have ever despaired over the size and complexity of our problems today, then hear this good news: God is going to exert a final authority that will change the world in a way that no human effort possibly could.

Our confidence in this ultimate outcome, however, does not mean we just shrug our shoulders at current problems and wait for the cosmic rescue vehicle to arrive. On the contrary, Jesus charged his disciples with being witnesses to this ultimate redemption by participating in the renewal of the world now. As we learned in chapter one, throughout the course of history Christ has used his followers to bring about dramatic renewal in many spheres of societal life. As we'll explore further in chapter ten, the most winsome witnesses will be those who model this world-renewing work and invite others to come participate in it.

5. You can enjoy life beyond death (resurrection). The gospel is also spectacularly good news for all of us who shake with sadness or quake with fear in the face of the *death issue*. "I am the resurrection and the life," said Jesus. "Anyone who believes in me will live, even though they die" (John 11:25 TNIV). The promise of Jesus is that those who put their hand into his hand in this life don't ever need to be afraid of dying. They don't need to grieve the death of fellow believers, as those who are without hope (1 Thessalonians 4:13-18).

For Christ assures us that, on the last day, he will raise up his followers to a staggering new life. "In the twinkling of an eye . . . the dead will be raised imperishable." God will give us an entirely new kind of body, no longer subject to decay, clothed with immortality. Death, our old enemy, will be swallowed up in the victorious power of Christ's eternal life (1 Corinthians 15:42-57; Philippians 3:20-21). As witnesses, then, we have the privilege of bearing to others the marvelous news, "If you will put your hand into the hand of Christ, you can enjoy life beyond the grave" (see, e.g., Luke 23:43).

You can love with the greatest love of all (glorification). If eternal life meant, as it is commonly thought, today's quality of life in infinite quantity, some of us might not sign up. Part of the reason for this is the *love issue* we examined earlier. Love is too little in too many places. But the message of the Bible is good news in one more amazing sense. Not only will we be given glorious new bodies on the day of resurrection; we will also be given entirely transformed hearts and a life of absolute love. The apostle Paul bears witness to this when he says, "I consider that our present sufferings are not worth comparing with the glory that will be revealed in us. . . . [For] those [Christ] justified, he also glorified" (Romans 8:18, 30). The apostle John fills out this picture when he says, "How great is the love the Father has lavished on us, that we should be called children of God!" (1 John 3:1). John is expressing the doctrine of justification. But Paul tells us that the news is even better than that. "But we know that when he appears, we shall be like him, for we shall see him as he is" (1 John 3:2). This is glorification.

God's nature is perfect love (1 Corinthians 13; 1 John 4:8). Those whose lives are rooted and established in God grow in his love while they are on earth (Ephesians 3:14-19). They are strengthened by his love to face without fear whatever challenges might have previously threatened their sense of identity or security (1 John 4:18). They can begin to love other people at a much more remarkable level than has become regular in this life (Ephesians 3:20).

But the best is yet to be. One day we will stand with Jesus face-to-face and forevermore. We will behold the magnificent glory of his perfect love and, like a great magnet imputing its properties to a lesser metal drawn near, Christ's character will become fully ours. "We shall be like him" (1 John 3:2). We will be gloriously loving beings, caught up in the eternal splendor of an unbroken love relationship with God and all who inhabit his kingdom (John 14:21, 23). This is the good news to which we bear witness.

NEWS YOU CAN USE

Do you understand a bit better now why the apostle Paul would write, "I am not ashamed of the gospel, because it is the power of God for the salvation of everyone who believes: first for the Jew, then for the Gentile" (Romans 1:16)? Do you grasp a bit more fully why he was willing to walk thousands of miles, endure great privation, and suffer punishment for the sake of this news (2 Corinthians 11:23-28)? Paul saw the gospel as much more than a personal spirituality for one tribe or nation. He saw it for what it truly is—the hope for salvation from all of the *issues* that have plagued the creation since the beginning of human history (Colossians 1:15-23).

As a Jew, Paul had been among the first to receive the message of God's saving love and it had begun to transform him. His passion now was to share this truth with the Gentiles—those who hadn't yet taken in the power of this message (Acts 26:4-18; 1 Corinthians 15:1-9). This is the way the gospel spreads. Someone takes in the wonder of the life and light and love of God and then wants to share this blessing with others. First it is in you, and then it flows out of you. First it is news to you, and then it becomes news you can use to help others.

Who in your circle of acquaintance is struggling with the daily news? Who might be richly blessed to know that they can

- Get right with God?
- Overcome their character flaws?
- Set their course by reliable truth?
- Participate in renewing this world?
- Enjoy life beyond death?
- Love with the greatest love of all?

This is the GOSPEL of salvation in the fullest sense. It is this grand hope that we take in our hearts and hands as we go forth as witnesses of Jesus Christ and his kingdom. Far from being ashamed of it, we are eager to share it. Why? I trust you can answer that question even more fully now. It is because anyone who really examines it can readily see that it is not just one spiritual message among many. The gospel is the greatest news ever shared.

---

[1]"Theologians: Barth in Retirement," *Time Magazine*, May 31, 1963.
[2]Mark Twain, *Tom Sawyer: Detective* (New York: Tom Doherty Associates, 1993), p. 2.

Application Exercise

1. Why do you think it is necessary for Christian witnesses to have a grasp of both the daily news (the newspaper) and the divine news (the gospel)?

2. Of the various *issues* the reading suggested shape the daily news, which do you recognize as especially significant to you or the people you meet?

   ☐ The Core Issue

   ☐ The Character Issue

   ☐ The Truth Issue

   ☐ The Change Issue

   ☐ The Mortality Issue

   ☐ The Love Issue

3. Draw a line between the theological concept (on the left) and the dimension of the good news (on the right) to which it relates.

Theological Concept:	The Good News is that you can:
Sanctification	**G**et right with God
Redemption	**O**vercome your character flaws
Glorification	**S**et your course by reliable truth
Resurrection	**P**articipate in renewing this world
Justification	**E**njoy life beyond death
Revelation	**L**ove with the greatest love of all

4. As you consider the various dimensions of the GOSPEL message described in the acronym above, which of them have made the most difference in your life so far and how?

5. Which of these dimensions of the GOSPEL do you sense you need to think about or live into further as you go forward?

6. Complete this sentence: "The good news our world especially needs to hear is . . ."

Going Deeper

Lewis, C. S. *Mere Christianity*. New York: HarperCollins, 2001.
Little, Paul E. *Know What You Believe*. Downers Grove, IL: InterVarsity Press, 2003.
Stott, John. *Basic Christianity*. Downers Grove, IL: InterVarsity Press, 2006.

3 / Mourn the Changed Conditions

LOOKING AHEAD

MEMORY VERSE: Isaiah 40:8
BIBLE STUDY: John 12:20-36
READING: Christendom Is Dead. Long Live the Kingdom!

 Core Truth

What is the context for Christian witness in the Western world?

Many disciples today find themselves in a period of glorious insecurity. While we may grieve the death of all the apparently advantageous arrangements that "Christendom" brought us, we are being compelled toward that state of blessed dependence upon God out of which can be born a new first-century faith.

1. Identify key words or phrases in the question and answer above, and state their meaning in your own words.

2. Restate the core truth in your own words.

3. What questions or issues does the core truth raise for you?

Memory Verse Study Guide

Copy the entire text here:

_____

_____

_____

_____

_____

_____

_____

_____

_____

_____

_____

_____

_____

_____

_____

_____

_____

_____

_____

_____

Memory Verse: Isaiah 40:8

The Old Testament prophets had repeatedly warned the Israelites of God's coming judgment on them for their faithlessness. With the conquest of Israel by the Assyrians and the Babylonians (722 and 586 B.C., respectively), the Israelites' king, temple and way of life were swept away and the surviving Jews sent into exile. Amidst this season, when all they'd foolishly counted on had died, the faith of Israel began to be born again. In Isaiah 40, the prophet proclaims comfort to his mourning people and the promise that God is about to do something new.

1. *Putting it in context:* Read Isaiah 40:1-11. What is the overall emotion of this passage and what specific words convey that?

2. Why do you suspect God let the Israelites experience the massive reversal of fortunes that their conquest and exile occasioned?

3. What parallels do you see between the story of the people of Israel during that season of history and the condition of the church in our time?

4. What is the assurance that is being communicated in the contrast Isaiah makes between the grass and flowers (v. 7) and the Word of the Lord (v. 8)?

5. What is the listener supposed to do with this good news and why (vv. 9-11)?

6. How have these verses spoken to you?

THE LONGER A PERSON LIVES, THE MORE HE OR SHE TENDS TO DWELL ON THE PAST RATHER THAN LIVE IN DYNAMIC INTERACTION WITH THE PRESENT OR BE INSPIRED BY THE HOPE OF FUTURE POSSIBILITIES. IF THIS IS TRUE FOR THE INDIVIDUAL, IT ALSO HOLDS TRUE FOR INSTITUTIONS THAT HAVE AN INHERENT CORPORATE CULTURE REINFORCED BY EACH SUCCEEDING GENERATION.

Eddie Gibbs

Inductive Bible Study Guide

Bible Study: John 12:20-36

Death is something from which most of us naturally run. In our Bible study passage, however, Jesus puts a new spin on death that is important to consider as we reflect in this chapter on what has happened to the world where many Christians (especially Western ones) are called to be witnesses.

1. *Read John 12:20-36.* In verses 23-24, what does Jesus imply is going to happen to him?

2. How does what Jesus says in verses 27-28 further display his attitude toward what is going to happen?

3. What will be the benefits of what is coming (vv. 24, 31-32)? List as many as you can.

4. This passage is talking specifically about the redeeming effects of Christ's death, but in verses 25-26 Jesus suggests that death will also be part of the experience of those who follow him. To what do the followers of Jesus also need to die?

5. What have you personally "died to" in the course of being a follower of Jesus?

6. As you consider the way the church in the West has done its work over the past fifty years and more, what may need to die so that new life can be born? (If you struggle to answer this, then return to this question after you've done the reading.)

Reading: Christendom Is Dead. Long Live the Kingdom!

THE MOST FAVORED PEOPLE

Think for a moment about what we've covered thus far: You and I are heirs of a centuries-long legacy of remarkably positive influence in this world. In spite of all her admitted flaws, no movement in history has done more to advance the well-being of humanity than the church of Jesus. No message contains greater capacity to transform human nature from the center, to alter human culture for the better or to secure human destiny forever than the gospel of the kingdom of God.

Given this background, we might reasonably expect followers of Jesus to be the most revered members of any society they inhabit. We should anticipate people approaching us regularly, eager to know more of the Christian message and life. One would think that most congregations and campus fellowships would be struggling to keep up with the torrents of inquirers flowing into their gatherings.

This was the experience of the early church. The book of Acts reports that Christ's witnesses then "enjoyed the favor of all the people" such that "the Lord added to their number daily those who were being saved" (Acts 2:42, 47). This is still the experience described by believers in many parts of the globe today (see chap. 1). For many of us in the West, however, this is not our experience and hasn't been for quite a long time.[1]

TAKE STOCK OF OUR LOSSES

While it is painful to face this reality, taking stock of the present conditions in which the church operates is a crucial step for would-be witnesses. Only after we've honestly mourned our losses will we be in a position to seize the fresh opportunities before us now.

1. Lost status. There was a time when churches and their members were regarded as among the greatest assets in any community. Local pastors were highly respected figures. Newspapers carried transcripts of Sunday sermons. Being an officer of a local church enhanced someone's credibility with others. When a church

> THE COMBINED IMPACT OF THE INFORMATION AGE, POSTMODERN THOUGHT, GLOBALIZATION, AND RACIAL-ETHNIC PLURALISM THAT HAS SEEN THE DEMISE OF THE GRAND AMERICAN STORY ALSO HAS DISPLACED THE HISTORIC ROLE THE CHURCH HAS PLAYED IN THAT STORY. AS A RESULT, WE ARE SEEING THE MARGINALIZATION OF THE INSTITUTIONAL CHURCH.
>
> Mike Regele with Mark Schulz

building was being constructed or expanded, most neighbors were very pleased. When a community faced pressing problems, Christian leaders were among the first consulted to help shape solutions.

In few places is this still true. The opinion of Christian leaders is not only rarely sought but frequently discouraged from open expression in public life. Listen to a celebrity express faith in Christ during an interview and watch how quickly the subject gets changed. Many of the difficult problems of our age are driven by *issues* to which Christians could helpfully speak. The themes explored on daytime talk shows and the immense popularity of religious books and websites all suggest that many people remain interested in spiritual matters. Nevertheless, representatives of Christianity are seldom asked to play a part in that discussion. Churches are increasingly regarded as irrelevant by many people. In some cases, they are viewed as liabilities within a community—a deplorable source of traffic congestion or tax-base erosion.

2. Lost significance. There was also a lengthy period when the Christian worldview was widely acknowledged as foundational to the development and continuance of Western culture. In a speech at Harvard University in 1829, U.S. Supreme Court justice Joseph Story, a man regarded as the Father of American Jurisprudence, declared: "There never has been a period in which the Common Law did not recognize Christianity as lying at its foundations. . . . I verily believe Christianity necessary to the support of civil society."[2] Numerous books have conclusively detailed the broad extent to which this view was shared by the American nation's founders and many of its most prominent leaders, well into the twentieth century.[3] Even after churches and their leaders lost their former stature, the Judeo-Christian ethic itself was generally accepted as fundamental to the health of public life.

As Yale Law School professor Stephen Carter has extensively documented, however, this day is long past. Those who hold the reigns of influence in the media, law and politics increasingly operate out of a "culture of disbelief,"[4] marginalizing, discounting or lampooning the Christian faith. That a code as broad, benign and universally recognized as the Ten Commandments is now banished from public display is a luminous indicator

> IT IS NOW TOO LATE TO TREAT WESTERN SOCIETY AS IN SOME SORT OF DECLINE FROM CHRISTIAN STANDARDS, TO BE BROUGHT BACK TO CHURCH BY PREACHING AND PERSUASION. MODERN WESTERN SOCIETY, TAKEN AS A WHOLE, REFLECTS ONE OF THE GREAT NON-CHRISTIAN CULTURES OF THE WORLD.
>
> Andrew Walls

of the extent to which the Judeo-Christian vision has lost its perceived significance. At every election time there is a resurgence of politicians who do some "chattering about the Lord."[5] They invoke the name of God and the principles of Christianity, but one gets the distinct impression that they are taking God's name in vain—using the rhetoric of faith to curry votes or endorse an agenda that ignores significant parts of the biblical witness.

3. *Lost influence.* Whatever their understanding of the appropriate relationship between church and state, cultures in the West were nourished for centuries by a biblical stream. Children learned to read using Bible primers. Mothers needle-pointed Scripture verses and posted them on family walls. Even the most irreligious persons were very familiar with the stories of the Bible, the teachings of Jesus, the admonitions of Paul. Allusions to biblical themes filled the artwork, literature and music of Europe and the Americas alike for centuries. Whether someone went to a church building on the weekend or not, few people could help but be shaped by the message of God's Word. It was the water in which people swam.

Today, these same cultures are scripturally desiccated and biblically illiterate. This fact was famously revealed by long-time American talk-show host Jay Leno in an interview with his audience. When asked to name one of the Ten Commandments, his first respondent struggled to come up with anything, then answered: "God helps those who help themselves"

(the maxim of Benjamin Franklin). The audience members could easily list the four members of the Beatles, but not a single person in the crowd could identify the name of one of the apostles. Most people had heard of Adam, Abraham, David, Solomon and Jesus, but few could put them in the correct chronological order.[6]

A study by the Gallup organization found that 63 percent of American teens could not correctly identify a quotation from the Sermon on the Mount ("Blessed are the poor in spirit, for theirs is the kingdom of heaven"). Two-thirds didn't know that the Road to Damascus was where St. Paul was blinded by a vision of Christ and converted to Christianity. And, perhaps even more sobering, those who self-identified as "born-again" or "evangelical" Christians were only slightly more likely to have the correct answer.[7]

The ultimate impact of this biblical illiteracy was displayed vividly in a landmark study headed up by Christian Smith of Notre Dame on the religious attitudes of American youth.[8] Smith and his colleagues found that 75 percent of teens today believe in God and remain very concerned with spiritual matters. Two-thirds of today's students, however, hold a view of God and life that Smith termed "moralistic therapeutic deism." It is *moralistic*, in that they believe that our ultimate standing before God depends upon our ability to rack up moral merit badges that will impress him. It is *therapeutic*, in that students believe that God's primary desire (or job) is to make them happy. And it is *deistic*, in that teens are persuaded that God is somewhere "out there" but not personally active in their life.

Conversely, the New Testament teaches that we are saved not by our works, but through God's grace embraced by faith (Romans 5:1-8; Ephesians 2:1-9). The Scriptures say that God's primary desire is the fulfillment of his kingdom, even if that requires the painful reshaping of our character and the postponement of our joy (Philippians 2:1-18). The Bible maintains that God is not a distant deity but an ever-present shepherd, very involved in human life (Matthew 6:24-25; 18:20; Hebrews 13:5). The pervasive ignorance of these once widely understood truths is further evidence of the extent to which a genuinely biblical worldview has lost influence in our day.

4. Lost trust. Throughout its history, the Christian movement has ebbed and flowed in its capacity to inspire trust among the people of its society. Revivals of faith have been fueled in certain seasons by the obvious credibility of Christ's disciples. Christian organizations like the Salvation Army and the Red Cross have been among the most trusted institutions in the world. Many pastors and priests have earned a reputation of integrity that has made people willing to share with them their most sensitive secrets and difficult problems.

At the same time, it can't be denied that Christianity today faces a significant crisis of trust among many people. A recent nationwide poll found that Americans feel greater trust in the military, small businesses, colleges, the Supreme Court and the medical community than they do in organized religion. Only 30 percent of the people surveyed expressed confidence in the practitioners of institutional religion.[9]

As we touched on in chapter one, some of this crisis of confidence has to do with the memory of very old wrongs. At times, certain Christians have shown a spectacular disregard for biblical precepts in their treatment of others. When the world needed them (and Christ called them) to stand up, they lay down, remained silent or actually twisted biblical teaching to suit selfish purposes.

This is not, however, just ancient history. The recent failure of the church to discipline and dismiss sexual predators from their ranks or even come clean about this failure has been devastating. The repeated revelation of profound ethical lapses by preachers well known for their critique of others' moral choices has done staggering damage. The witness of televangelists who wring money from the poor while living lives of extravagant excess themselves has for many people shattered the credibility of the Christian God and his gospel.

People also notice it when Christians can't seem to get along with one another and when churches split. They take mental notes when they see alleged disciples claiming Christ when it is convenient and living any way they choose when it isn't. When "believers" speak of a "God who so loved the world" but then can't seem to love their own family members very well, observers are affected. When they see Christians exhibiting a stunning lack of charity and civility toward those who differ with them, it hurts their trust in the salvation we proclaim.

5. *Lost numbers.* It is well known now that church attendance in Britain and Europe has, for many years, been very low.[10] In light of the factors we've explored above, one might expect the American experience to be heading in this direction too. Surprisingly, recent Gallup polls suggest that perhaps the American experience is defying this downward trend. Gallup reports that weekly attendance in the United States is relatively stable, hovering at 42 to 45 percent.[11]

Before we comfort ourselves too quickly, however, even this statistic has to be assessed in terms of the "halo effect"—the proven tendency of people to give answers that make them appear better to the pollster. A far more reliable indicator of actual behavior is what churches themselves report in terms of actual head counts at weekend services. Here, the numbers tell a very different story. The data indicates that real church attendance is only about 17 percent of the population and is declining by close to 2 percent every decade. This is in spite of

YOU ARE A CHOSEN PEOPLE, A ROYAL PRIESTHOOD, A HOLY NATION, A PEOPLE BELONGING TO GOD, THAT YOU MAY DECLARE THE PRAISES OF HIM WHO CALLED YOU OUT OF DARKNESS INTO HIS WONDERFUL LIGHT. ONCE YOU WERE NOT A PEOPLE, BUT NOW YOU ARE THE PEOPLE OF GOD.

1 Peter 2:9-10

continued population growth. At this rate, it is estimated that by 2050 only 10 percent of Americans will be in church on any given Sunday.[12] There will still be many vital smaller churches, and very likely an increasing consolidation of existing believers into the multiple-service megachurches rising on the landscape. But this is a long way from the picture of a Christian movement where "the Lord added to their number daily those who were being saved" (Acts 2:47).

6. *Lost martyrdom.* As already stated in chapter one, the place and picture of the church around the globe is dramatically more encouraging than this in some respects.[13] But we dare not forget how greatly our brothers and sisters in other parts of the planet have sacrificed in order to gain the spiritual clarity, vitality and influence they are now enjoying. Before we in the West indulge too deeply in a pity party, it behooves us to remember that the English word "witness" comes from the Greek word *martyr.* Jesus told his disciples that following him would require a willingness to carry a cross, not a comfy chair. He explained that entering his kingdom would involve the sacrifice of many of the securities that this world holds most dear (Luke

18:18-25). He assured us that if the world persecuted and rejected him, we should expect it to reject us too at times (John 15:20). Christ taught that if he was to be fully born in us, then we should be prepared to die to ourselves (Luke 9:23-25).

Yes, Christians in the West have been suffering a progressive loss of status, significance, influence, trust and numbers. This is, understandably, upsetting. But measure these losses against the sacrifice of family, jobs, homes and life itself that many witnesses around the world are willing to endure for the sake of the gospel. Consider the possibility that our losses actually invite us to depend on God and one another in the way that our brothers and sisters around the globe learned long ago. Maybe it is time to grieve our losses and then move on.

Grieve the Loss

In her celebrated book *On Death and Dying*, Elisabeth Kubler-Ross set out what are now widely accepted as the five stages of grief.[14] When someone suffers a painful loss, he or she will tend to move along a somewhat predictable path that embraces the experience of (1) denial, (2) anger, (3) bargaining, (4) depression and (5) acceptance. People don't always move through these stages in this exact order. They may jump back and forth or get stuck for awhile. But, if they keep moving, they will emerge—in spite of all they've lost—to a place where life begins afresh.

Many Western Christians are in the midst of this grieving process today.

What has died is not the hope of the gospel, the relevance of the Christian message or the capacity of Jesus to transform lives, churches and whole societies. What is dead is that former arrangement of things that used to go by the name "Christendom."

Christendom was the world where Christians were recognized as the powerful majority, where their values were the espoused values of the society around them, and where the major institutions of the culture (governments, courts, schools, arts, families and churches) collaborated, at least nominally, in reinforcing those values. As long as Christendom existed, followers of Christ felt fundamentally central and validated.

This arrangement has now died. Christians still have a voice in the society—an extraordinarily important voice—but they are not speaking softly and confidently from the center so much as shouting somewhat anxiously from the margins, straining to be heard. The society's values have shifted and, in many ways, bear little practical resemblance to biblical values. The institutions of culture nod to Christianity in places but no longer collaborate to uphold it. In many ways they ignore it or oppose it.

This, I contend, is the new reality with which we must reckon. Understandably, however, many people are not ready to do this. Coping with the death of someone or something you loved—that gave you a sense of security, identity and influence—is not easy.

Denial. Some Christians today are at the denial stage of the grieving process. They won't or they can't yet take in that a death has occurred. Christendom may be a bit sick, they maintain, but certainly not gone. In the words of the old Monty Python sketch, they look at the rigor mortis that has set into the parrot of once-popular Christianity and they keep repeating, "It's not dead. It's resting." People in this place go on about their faith with a stolid conviction that the society will wake up any day now and return to the way it was. Our job as Christians, they feel, is to just keep doing what we've always done, the way we've always done it. Just keep hanging out the church sign and keep the doors open. Things will get better.

Anger. There are others, however, who are not as placid. "We've all got to get good and mad at the way things are going," they say. "We've got to rise up and tell these wing-nuts in Washington and Hollywood that we're not going to let them hijack our country. We've got to go on the attack and let these atheists and amoralists know that we're not going to take it anymore." People at the anger stage focus a lot of energy on all the enemies of Christianity and very little on self-reflection. If we just get mad and motivated enough, we can roll back the clock. If we just start making church the way it was when we grew up, we can put things back the way they were.

Bargaining. Then there are those at the bargaining stage. They are willing to look at themselves and the way they've been doing the faith, but only at a surface level.

"Maybe if we just accommodate the culture a bit more, we can get our place back at the center of this society. Perhaps if we allow some of that new music into our worship services, or avoid those passages in the Bible that challenge the way people use money, or accept more pieces of that evolution idea, then people will want to come join us again." The thinking is that if we can only downplay all that sin talk that upsets people or ramp up more of that entertainment that enthralls people, the church can reclaim its place of centrality in the world. Or, at the very least, my neighbors and friends won't think I'm weird or some kind of fool.

Depression. Some people, however, know that this won't work. They can't deny anymore that the conditions have changed. They may have been angry for a season, but they saw that it gave them no more influence on the people they'd like to see come to faith or church than the Pharisees had. Perhaps they tried bargaining for a while. Then they realized that this meant watering down truths that will always seem scandalous or uncomfortable to non-disciples until God fills their core (1 Corinthians 1:18). They saw that if all you do is keep catering to the culture you may succeed in drawing more consumers, but not in making more Christians.

But they can't yet see what a better way looks like. They don't have a picture of how Christianity could once again be the fabulous force it ought to be given its remarkable historical record, its wonderful gospel and its marvelous Lord. Surrounded by so many evidences of loss, all they feel is the weight of dead or dying faith. They feel very depressed and terribly sad.

BEGIN ANEW

Many years ago, I felt a sadness something like that. A fellow pastor and I had journeyed with a group from our church to western Turkey, retracing the footsteps of the apostle Paul. One afternoon all of us were standing waist-high among the golden grasses of a rolling field. As my colleague Ed led our devotions, I stripped off a handful of seed-heads from those grasses and rolled them in the palm of my hand. Ed was reading from Paul's letter to the Colossians and we were standing right there where the town of Colossae once had been. All that was left now was a grassy mound where the church had once been—just an empty field where the gospel once thrived. I thought of all the cities we'd seen where disciples once walked and the Word of God once rang. All of this, now in ruins and silent. "Where did your Life go, God?" I asked. "How did you let your witness die?"

And then it happened.

A breeze came up and swept across that golden field, catching up the heads of the grasses like I'd taken up those seeds in my hand. It sent thousands, maybe millions, of seeds flying with the wind to go rest and root in some other place. Suddenly, the words of the Scriptures came thundering into my mind: "The grass withers and the flowers fall, but the word of our God stands forever" (Isaiah 40:8). "I tell you the truth," said Jesus, "unless a kernel of wheat falls to the ground and dies, it remains only a single seed. But if it dies, it produces many seeds" (John 12:24).

Acceptance. Sometimes something must die in order for something far greater to be born. Christendom is no more in Turkey. It is fading or dead in the West today. But this does not mean that God is done sowing the seeds of eternal life. I serve a congregation in North America that is thousands of believers strong. We are the heirs of the seed once planted at Colossae, and there are millions, even billions, more such offshoots now. One good look at the Pando-like explosion of Christian life in fields around the planet today, and this will become clear: the Great Sower is still very much at work.

Reggie McNeal says that we in the West have got to get past our grief over the way things have changed in our context. We've got to stop thinking about turning the page back. "You're not going to find GOD going *back* anywhere," says McNeal. "God is always coming to us from the future."[15] God isn't surprised by the conditions we face today. He saw this day coming and it did not worry him. Why? Because he actually specializes in taking death and bringing forth from it new life. "When I am lifted up . . . [I] will draw all people to myself" (John 12:32 TNIV), said Jesus.

WELCOME TO THE NEW FIRST CENTURY

So let's forget about being maintainers of our old place in a post-Christendom society and start learning again from Jesus, his first disciples, and martyrs (witnesses) outside the West today what it is to be missionaries in a pre-Christian society. Again, Reggie McNeal puts it bluntly and well:

> The death of the church culture as we know it will not be the death of the church. The church Jesus founded is good; it is right. The church established by Jesus will survive until he returns. The demise under discussion is the collapse of the unique culture in America that has come to be called "church." This church culture has become confused with biblical Christianity, both inside the church and out. In reality, the church culture in North America is a vestige of the original movement, an institutional expression of religion that is in part a civil religion and in part a club where religious people can hang out with other people whose politics, worldview, and lifestyle match theirs. As he hung on the cross Jesus probably never thought the impact of his sacrifice would be reduced to an invitation for people to join and to support an institution.[16]

It is time for us to rediscover what it means to be a missional church instead of merely a church with a missions budget. We need to surrender our efforts to preserve a monument to the past and give ourselves instead to advancing the movement of the future. We must stop expecting people to suddenly decide to come into our buildings and start taking the

life and message of Jesus out "into all the world" (Mark 16:15). As hard as it may be for some of us to take in, the demise of the former arrangements is not bad news at all. As author John Updike reminds us: "Growth is betrayal of arrangements that were; growth is change that is threatening as well as promising; growth is denial of something and affirmation of something else; growth is dangerous and glorious insecurity."[17]

We now find ourselves at a moment in history where the conditions around us are remarkably like the ones in which the vital faith and phenomenal expansion of the first church was born:

- Like our earliest spiritual forebears, we cannot expect the government or society to prop us up or do our work for us. Once we get over our grief about this, this new reality can become for us, as it was for them, a wonderful opportunity to be a truly distinctive people, dependent upon God alone.

- As in the first century, the twenty-first century is a time when many people are wearying of the decadence of a waning empire and equally wary of legalistic religion. They are every bit as open to hearing of a God who offers them a healthier life, but need to know that following him is about more than joining another narrow club or enslaving themselves to a new set of life-choking laws.

- Amidst a milieu of growing pluralism, tribalism and cultural conflict similar to that of the first century, many now—as then—are looking for a worldview that wisely interprets our problems and brings people together behind a new understanding of community and responsibility.

- While the majority of people today will have declining interest in religious institutions, they will be as fascinated by the person of Jesus as those in the first century were, if we can find ways of genuinely reflecting the glory of his life and love to them.

Yes, it is an admittedly poor time to be a citizen of Christendom; but it is a glorious time to be a witness to the all-surpassing power and goodness of the kingdom of God. That's the mission for which the next section of this book aims to start equipping you. Welcome to the New First Century of the Christian movement. Jesus says, "Join me here."

---

[1]Readers whose life context is outside the West (and the United States in particular) may find these next pages to be of greater academic interest than of practical application. This chapter of the book is aimed at the particular conditions faced by Western Christians today.

[2]William W. Story, ed., *Life and Letters of Joseph Story* (Boston: Charles C. Little and James Brown, 1851), 2:8, 92.

[3]David Barton, *America's Godly Heritage* (Aledo, TX: Wallbuilder Press, 1993).

[4]Stephen L. Carter, *The Culture of Disbelief: How American Law and Politics Trivialize Religious Devotion* (New York: HarperCollins, 1993).

[5]Stephen L. Carter, *God's Name in Vain: The Wrongs and Rights of Religion in Politics* (New York: Basic Books, 2000).

[6]Clayton Hardiman, "Final Answer: Bible Literacy Slipping," Amarillo.com, April 21, 2001.

[7]*The Bible Literacy Report* (Front Royal, VA: Bible Literacy Project, 2005).

[8]Christian Smith, "The National Study of Youth and Religion," *Resources for American Christianity,* www.resourcingchristianity.org/.

[9]Harris Poll as reported by MilitaryInfo.com, March 7, 2006.

[10]Nationmaster.com.

[11]"Americans' Church Attendance Inches Up," Gallup.com, June 25, 2010.

[12]David T. Olson, *The American Church in Crisis* (Grand Rapids: Zondervan, 2008).

[13]John Micklethwait and Adrian Wooldridge, *God Is Back: How the Global Revival of Faith Is Changing the World* (New York: Penguin, 2009).

[14]Elisabeth Kübler-Ross, *On Death and Dying* (New York: Macmillan, 1969).

[15]Reggie McNeal, "The Church in a Pre-Christian World," Oak Brook Conference on Ministry, November 7, 2003.

[16]Reggie McNeal, *The Present Future: Six Tough Questions for the Church* (San Francisco: Jossey-Bass, 2003), p. 1.

[17]Robert A. Raines, *To Kiss the Joy* (Waco, TX: Word, 1973), p. 116.

Application Exercise

1. What adjectives would you use to describe the state of Christianity in the West today?

2. The reading asserts that the Christian movement in the West has suffered some difficult losses in recent decades. Which of the various losses described do you see evidence of and how?

   ☐ Lost status—not valued or sought out

   ☐ Lost significance—no longer regarded as essential to society

   ☐ Lost influence—not shaping beliefs and behaviors to biblical vision

   ☐ Lost trust—no longer thought of as reliable by outsiders

   ☐ Lost numbers—not growing on the whole

   ☐ Lost martyrdom—not much willingness to behave sacrificially

3. The reading asserts that many Christians are in a state of mourning over the changed conditions in which the church now operates. How have you seen any of the following stages of grief being expressed by Christians today? Can you identify with any particular stage yourself?

   ☐ Denial:

   ☐ Anger:

   ☐ Bargaining:

   ☐ Depression:

   ☐ Acceptance:

4. How might these emotions (particularly the first four) affect the ability of Christians to be the witnesses needed in our time?

5. Does the reading convict, challenge or comfort you? Why?

Going Deeper

Gibbs, Eddie. *ChurchNext: Quantum Changes in How We Do Ministry*. Downers Grove, IL: InterVarsity Press, 2000.

McNeal, Reggie. *The Present Future: Six Tough Questions for the Church*. San Francisco: Jossey-Bass, 2003.

Part Two

REACHING OUT TO PEOPLE

We live in an age where speed and simplicity are all the rage. In the space of a television hour, we can see murder mysteries unraveled and difficult dramas resolved. With the whir of a microwave, we can quickly enjoy popcorn or lasagna. Everywhere around us are quick-start guides and ready-to-use gadgets promising super solutions in seven simple steps.

Not surprisingly, then, when it comes to sharing our faith with others, we tend to look for an approach that is similarly fast and easy. Just teach us the Roman Road to Salvation. Help us learn the Four Spiritual Laws. Equip us with the entertaining Christian video or the latest book to banish all doubts.

There is nothing wrong with "helps" like these. Having such tools and techniques can be genuinely useful at some point in our conversation with people. For many decades these trusted approaches often worked well in helping nondisciples begin an intentional journey with Jesus. But in this new first century of the Christian movement, a different methodology is needed, especially at the start—one much closer to the way the gospel spread when our movement first began. That approach is what this part of the book seeks to describe.

Yearn for People as God Does (chap. 4). We begin this section by examining the yearning heart that Jesus displayed toward nondisciples. The average person today will not be very interested in giving a fresh hearing to the Christian message until he or she trusts the heart of the messenger. We'll take a hard look at the bad experiences many people have had with the "God of religion" and see how we can better represent the "God of relationship" whose love longs to find lost people and bless them richly at the place of their deepest needs.

Walk with People (chap. 5). Next, we'll explore what it looks like to walk with people as Jesus did. Christ deeply valued the life of the spiritual community that was his foundation, but his passion was for the mission field, and his focus was on the people who walked out there. Our energies must be similarly directed outward toward building redemptive relationships with people in the places where they feel at home. We'll discover together some specific keys to doing this.

Investigate and Invest in the Soil (chap. 6). Finally, we'll reflect on the work of "spiritual agriculture" as Jesus revealed it. Effective evangelism requires a clear understanding of God's role and ours in the process of bringing someone to faith. We'll look at the various kinds of spiritual soil we meet in the people around us. We'll then consider how to start cultivating the ground for significant spiritual conversations with others and the extraordinary fruit that can ultimately come from this kind of careful investment.

4 / Yearn for People as God Does

MEMORY VERSE: Luke 19:10
BIBLE STUDY: Luke 15:1-32
READING: Lost and Found

 **Core Truth**

What is the heart we need to bring to our work as Christ's witnesses?

God wants his disciples to be dramatically different from the representatives of religion who have increased the resistance of many to the claims of the Christian faith. He calls us to be filled with his good heart toward people, to yearn relentlessly to see lost people found by his love, and to help others discover the multiple blessings that a relationship with Christ alone can give.

1. Identify key words or phrases in the question and answer above, and state their meaning in your own words.

> PEOPLE CAN ONLY BE
>
> LOVED INTO THE KINGDOM.
>
> J. B. Phillips

2. Restate the core truth in your own words.

3. What questions or issues does the core truth raise for you?

Memory Verse Study Guide

Copy the entire text here:

_____

_____

_____

_____

_____

_____

_____

_____

_____

_____

_____

_____

_____

_____

_____

_____

_____

_____

_____

Memory Verse: Luke 19:10

While many public figures exert great energy rushing around and trying to address the largest possible audience, Jesus more often did the opposite. He lingers to talk with a lone Samaritan woman, stops by a roadside to listen to the troubles of a blind beggar and turns to engage a bleeding person who'd touched him in a crowd. In our Memory Verse passage, too, we see the profound value Jesus places on loving individuals.

1. *Putting it in context: Read Luke 19:1-9.* What do these verses suggest about the popularity of Jesus at this point in his ministry?

2. What do you learn about Zacchaeus from this passage?

3. What is the crowd's response to Jesus' interest in Zacchaeus and why (v. 7)?

4. In what sense could this wealthy man be regarded as "lost" (v. 9)?

5. What seems to be the emotion or attitude of Jesus toward Zacchaeus (vv. 5-9)?

6. How would you put in your own words Jesus' mission statement (v. 10)?

MISSIONARY ZEAL DOES NOT GROW OUT OF INTELLECTUAL BELIEFS, NOR OUT OF THEOLOGICAL ARGUMENTS, BUT OUT OF LOVE.

Roland Allen

Inductive Bible Study Guide

Bible Study: Luke 15:1-32

The passage in this study further reveals the depths of God's yearning love for those who are living apart from him and the lengths to which he'll go to close this distance. Jesus emphasizes this reality by telling four successive stories. All of these parables illustrate some very important elements of the backdrop against which the work of Christian witness is done.

1. *Read Luke 15:1-2.* Who are the two audiences listening in as Jesus teaches in this passage and what do you suppose their attitude toward Jesus is?

2. *Read Luke 15:4-24.* What are the common elements in these three stories? List as many as you can find.

3. What are the potential risks or real losses associated with the missing items in each story?

   a. The lost sheep—

b. The lost coin—

c. The lost son—

4. If the main character in each story represents God, what does this say about how he views those who are separated from him?

5. *Read Luke 15:25-32.* In what way is the elder brother in the fourth story also "lost"?

6. What questions or issues does this passage raise for you?

Reading: Lost and Found

When Jesus walked onto the stage of history in the first century, the old way of doing religion had reached a dead end. It was remarkably similar to the conditions that would be faced by his followers at the close of Christendom twenty centuries later. If faith in God was to catch fire among ordinary people, they had to be given a vision of God dramatically different from their experience with the typical representatives of religion. Jesus embodied that heart—the same one still needed today.

THE GOD OF RELIGION

As in our time, first-century Palestine had plenty of religious people. There was an entire caste of "Pharisees" and "teachers of the law" (sometimes called "scribes") who considered themselves very committed to advancing the concerns of God (Luke 5:21). They went to a place of worship regularly and were always there on the big holy days. They carefully observed a long list of religious do's and don'ts. They scrupulously avoided being stained by contact with the dirty things of this world. They had memorized long swaths of Scripture, knew their doctrines well and could speak with eloquence about God.

This kind of "righteousness" did not impress Jesus favorably (Matthew 5:20). On the contrary, Christ reserved his harshest criticisms for these people, calling them hypocrites, sons of hell, blind guides, fools and serpents. He pronounced woe upon them and called them to change their hearts (Matthew 23:4-33). What was it about these people that so upset Jesus?

1. Haughtiness. For one thing, the Pharisees and teachers appear to have been immensely pretentious people. They made great, clanging contributions to the temple coffers, prayed long, loud prayers and suffered visibly through fasts. They made a spectacular show of their religion, telling themselves that they were doing all this to honor God and inspire others. Jesus asserted, however, that it was haughtiness, not holiness, at which these religious people excelled. Their acts were aimed at impressing other people or feeling superior to them (Matthew 6:1-16). This brand of "righteousness," however, not only drew few people toward God, it gave faith a bad name.

> ONE OF THE MOST REASSURING QUALITIES OF GOD IS THAT HE NEVER GIVES UP ON US. HE PURSUES US AND HE WILL SEEK US UNTIL WE DRAW OUR LAST BREATH. FOR IT IS GOD'S DEEPEST DESIRE THAT NO ONE PERISH. . . . WHEN WE FINALLY TURN TO HIM, WHAT WE SEE ARE HIS EYES OF LOVE.
>
> Becky Pippert

2. Hypocrisy. The scribes and the Pharisees were also remarkably two-faced people. They talked about pleasing God and following his laws, but they were lying to themselves. They did not maintain the high standards they foisted on others. They were like "white-washed tombs," said Jesus, beautiful on the outside but rotting with self-indulgence and lawlessness within. When Jesus pointed out this hypocrisy, they not only refused to face it in themselves but decided to kill the messenger (Matthew 23:1-28; Mark 11:18). Ordinary people saw the inconsistencies between the proclamations and the actual practices of these religionists too. They naturally wondered: "How can these people save others when they so obviously need saving themselves?"

3. Hard-heartedness. It was, however, the third quality of the Pharisees and teachers that seems to have upset Jesus the most. The "religious" people of first-century Palestine were terribly hard-hearted toward others. Piling upon people's shoulders a crushing list of expectations, they seemed far more interested in seeing their superficial rituals and narrow prescriptions kept than in having hungry people fed, sick ones healed or outcasts recovered. Rather than advancing God's mission to protect the weak, help the poor, and spread mercy and justice, these religious people regarded those whose lives were broken in any way as disposable "sinners." They could not understand why Jesus welcomed such people (Matthew 23:1-28; Luke 15:1-2).

> OUR RESEARCH SHOWS THAT MANY OF THOSE OUTSIDE OF CHRISTIANITY, ESPECIALLY YOUNGER ADULTS, HAVE LITTLE TRUST IN THE CHRISTIAN FAITH, AND ESTEEM FOR THE LIFESTYLE OF CHRIST FOLLOWERS IS QUICKLY FADING . . . THEY ADMIT THEIR EMOTIONAL AND INTELLECTUAL BARRIERS GO UP WHEN THEY ARE AROUND CHRISTIANS, AND THEY REJECT JESUS BECAUSE THEY FEEL REJECTED BY CHRISTIANS.
>
> David Kinnaman

HOW PEOPLE VIEW RELIGION TODAY

Regrettably, the cult of the Pharisees and teachers did not die out in the first century. A friend who pastors a church in Reno, Nevada, regularly goes down to the town's notorious "strip" and interviews the people who emerge from the gambling houses and nightspots there. "What do you think of when you hear the word *Christian*?" he asks. Occasionally, the response is wonderfully positive: "My mom comes to mind," someone will say, eyes misting slightly. Or "I think of somebody who is very kind." More frequently the response is neutral: "Christianity is mostly an external label," one person declared. "It's like being from Iowa or having brown hair. It doesn't make all that much difference." Increasingly, however, people will come up with words like *conceited, hypocritical* or *judgmental.* Some even use the word *dangerous.*

Interviewees will go on to describe someone who cut them no slack or who gave them the impression that they were very aware of the moral lapses in others but were somehow blind to their own. They characterize religious people as trying to lay rules and regulations on others, as people who define life in terms of what they are *against* instead of what they are *for.* The overwhelming theme my friend hears is that Christians aren't people who *want good for others* so much as they are people who *want to feel good about themselves* by forcing their beliefs on other people. "I get the sense that they don't really want to listen to me or care for me," someone might say. "I'm not a unique person to them. I'm just a red target for their evangelistic efforts . . . a potential notch on their conversion belt . . . a 'sinner story' they can tell when they get back to church . . . a strike-zone for their ideology bomb."

If we're going to be effective witnesses today, we can't be perceived as being even remotely like this. If people get the feeling that our faith is mostly a cultural label that doesn't make much of a difference at all, our witness will mean nothing. If they get the sense that our faith is a tool we use to maintain a haughty superiority, to conceal our hypocrisy or to beat others into sub-

mission, our witness will only push people away. Nondisciples need to meet in us a heart a lot less like the Pharisees and teachers of the law and much more like Jesus.

And there lies the hope.

Most of the time, my friend in Reno will conclude his interviews by asking one more question: "What do you think of when you hear the word *Jesus*?" Almost without fail, the tone of the conversation changes and the respondent softens. "Jesus? Well, I *like* Jesus . . . I am attracted to him . . . I love his heart for people . . . I don't know if he was really God or just a very great man . . . I'm not even sure I believe in God. But, if there is a God, I hope he's like Jesus."

THE GOD OF RELATIONSHIP

When Christ came in the first century, the world had seen a lot of the "God of religion," but far too little of the "God of relationship." Overwriting this wrong impression would take time and, ultimately, the outpouring of God's own heart upon a cross. But Jesus patiently set about laying the groundwork that would enable some people to one day grasp the meaning of that final sacrifice and the heartbeat behind it.

One of the most potent ways Jesus did this was through the stories he told. On one occasion, "the tax collectors and 'sinners' were all gathering around to hear him" (Luke 15:1). To the Pharisees observing this encounter, Jesus was wasting his time with the equivalent of casino people. They began muttering to themselves,

"This man welcomes sinners and eats with them" (Luke 15:2). It was then that Jesus began to tell a string of illuminating stories (Luke 15:3-32). Each of these stories shares four important elements worth noting.

1. Something is missing. The first story Jesus tells is about a man who owns a hundred sheep. The second is about a woman who had ten silver coins. The third tale is about a father who had two sons. In each case, one of these possessions has gone missing, through no apparent fault of the owner. A sheep wanders off, obviously out of stupidity. A coin rolls away, perhaps as a result of innocent gravity. A son splits from his family too early in life, clearly out of selfish depravity. These sorts of things happen all the time and for the same reasons. Bad choices, blind chance and broken character result in a lot of the hurt and hardships of life.

2. Who cares for the lost? The second common element in these stories is the response of those who would have been listening to Jesus. Christ doesn't supply this soundtrack but it's not hard to fill in. The conventional response to each loss would likely have been: "Who cares?" "It serves that dumb sheep right if he becomes wolf-bait." To the woman they'd say: "Don't bother with the missing coin. It'll probably turn up at some point. Besides, you've got nine more pieces of silver and that's still a tidy sum." To the father they'd shout: "Let the kid starve! He's proven himself worthless by demanding his inheritance early. If he ever returns,

have him stoned." This is the dismissive or condemning way many people today regard those who have wandered into bad places or strayed far from God.

3. Someone cares deeply. It is the third element of each story that offers a genuine surprise. Leaving the other ninety-nine in "the open country," the shepherd ventures off into what was, implicitly, the more tangled countryside, searching high and low until he locates the missing lamb. Lighting a lamp and grabbing a broom, the woman goes knees-and-cheek-down to the floor, fishing around "carefully," under every object until she finds her coin. Seeing his boy "while he was still a long way off," the father forgets his dignity and past injury, hikes up his robe, and goes running out to meet his criminally errant son. Who else makes this kind of effort to find the lost?

4. Celebration. And, finally, in each story, a great party ensues. The shepherd "calls his friends and neighbors together and says, 'Rejoice with me; I have found my lost sheep.'" The woman in the second story gathers all her associates together and says, "Rejoice with me; I have found my lost coin." The father in the last tale cries to his servants, "Bring the fattened calf and kill it. Let's have a feast and celebrate. For this son of mine was dead and is alive again; he was lost and is found." In each case, a celebration is held that seems utterly out of proportion to the apparent value of the item. Clearly the chief celebrant in each story attributes very high value to what has been found.

GETTING THE HEART OF GOD

In telling these stories, Jesus is trying to help his audience get to know the profoundly loving heart of God toward even the very least and most lost people of this world. Some of the religious people listening would certainly have said, "I don't get it. Why be excited over the reclamation of a stupid sheep, an ordinary coin, a lousy son?" That Jesus anticipates this response is evident from the story he goes on to tell. He describes the reaction of the elder son to the news that his father is throwing a party for his wayward brother: "All these years I've been slaving for you and never disobeyed your orders. Yet you never gave me even a young goat so I could celebrate with my friends. But when this son of yours who has squandered your property with prostitutes comes home, you kill the fattened calf for him!" (Luke 15:29-30). Some churchgoing people feel similarly puzzled or angry when cer-tain disciples or leaders seem far more concerned about reaching the lost than honoring or caring for those who never wandered away.

> IT'S AS THOUGH JESUS IS SAYING TO HIS FOLLOWERS, "WHAT I DID AS I WALKED ACROSS THE COSMOS ALL THOSE YEARS AGO, I NOW WANT YOU TO DO. EVERY DAY, TRY TO POINT EVERY PERSON YOU MEET TO ME. LIVE AS THOUGH YOU ACTUALLY BELIEVE THAT YOUR PARENT, YOUR COWORKER, AND YOUR NEIGHBOR WOULD BE BETTER OFF IF THEY KNEW MY FATHER—IF THEY WERE ON THE RECEIVING END OF HIS COUNSEL, HIS WISDOM, AND HIS GUIDANCE. . . . BE PEOPLE WHO ARE WILLING TO SEIZE EVERY OPPORTUNITY I GIVE YOU—NOT MOTIVATED BY GUILT OR FEAR OR OBLIGATION, BUT JUST WITH AN EYE ON ME, A PLIABLE HEART, AND A PASSION FOR MY PEOPLE."
>
> Bill Hybels

CRAZY LOVE

God's grace, frankly, doesn't make sense from the conventional point of view. From the vantage point of religion, what matters most is doing the "right thing." It's the ones who stay in the fold, who remain in the purse, who don't stray from home that ought to be cherished. According to the "religious" framework (in contrast to the relational one), it's the people who faithfully frequent the temple (or church), whose rule-keeping seems sterling, who don't upset the natural order of things who ought to gain God's favor. But this perspective only demonstrates that "lost-ness" can take more than one form.

The fact that the elder brother sees himself as "slaving" for the father instead of serving him displays that he doesn't have a loving relationship with his dad. The fact that he resents not being given "even a young goat" shows that he doesn't value the privilege of dining with his father every day. The fact that he sees the wayward boy as "this son of yours" instead of as "this brother of mine" reveals that, in spite of all the time he's spent at the father's house, he still does not get what it means to be family.

The "elder brothers" of this world, like the religionists in every century, struggle to get the Father's heart. Their haughtiness, hypocrisy and hard-heartedness show that they—like the "younger sons" of this world—are also lost. As Tim Keller has said, the younger sons are separated from God by their selfishness, the elder ones by their self-righteousness. But both are living outside of a proper relationship with God. Each is in need of salvation.[1]

Thankfully, Jesus is this Savior. In the stories he tells, in the way he lives and dies, in the call he gives to his witnesses after his resurrection, Jesus shows us that God's heart beats with a relentless compassion for all who are lost. Jesus shows us that God will cross the open country, hack his way into the thicket and expose himself to injury to find lost people. He will stoop down from the heights of eternity, get on his knees and go cheek-down to the grimy ground of this earth to find lost people. God will scan the horizon every moment of every day and run to close the distance between himself and lost people. He will leave a party filled with angels and go outside into the darkness to draw back to his heart even those lost in religion (Luke 15:10, 28). Jesus tells us that God's yearning obsession is "to seek and to save what was lost" of every kind (Luke 19:10).

SIGNS OF LOSTNESS

That is very good news, because a lot of people today are lost in one way or another.

Loneliness. Garrison Keillor tells the story of sitting at the typewriter in his home while the strains of his son's electric guitar wafted down the stairs. The music the boy was playing was of the heavy-metal blues variety, and the chords tugged at his father's heart because they were "so wrenchingly sad." "Where did he learn that?" Keillor mused. "I give him enough money. I'm a nice dad. We get along well. He does well in school. . . . Where does he get this anguish?" And then Keillor adds: "I guess we all got it inside of us."[2]

That is increasingly true of life for many. People have many of the things they want. They have lots of nice relationships. They may do well by society's standards. But deep inside many people there play the painful chords of an anguished loneliness. When I'm privileged to talk with them in the counseling room, I hear beneath their words and sighs a longing for someone who truly knows them intimately, for someone who walks with them consistently, for someone who cares for them unconditionally. Many people ache at the absence of *true love*.

Meaninglessness. There are also those who long today for a genuine hope that seems missing. By hope I mean a set of worthy aspirations that fill life with purpose and confidence. It's the antidote to the sense of bored meaninglessness that afflicts so many today. One writer put it in these words: "People no longer seem to know why they are alive; existence is simply a string of near-experiences marked off by periods of stupefying spiritual and psychological stasis, and the good life is basically an amused one."[3] Those words were written by playwright Arthur Miller in 1962. Yet how much truer they are today. We've gone from being a purpose-driven culture to being an entertainment-driven society; from hoping we could help build something of God's kingdom on earth to hoping there's something good on the screen or in the fridge tonight.

The ancient commandments have been replaced by ten new ones: (1) Thou shalt have a good day. (2) Thou shalt shop. (3) Thou shalt eliminate pain. (4) Thou shalt be up-to-date. (5) Thou shalt relax and not feel guilty. (6) Thou shalt express thyself. (7) Thou shalt have a happy family. And the three final ones? (8) Thou shalt be entertaining, (9) be entertained, and (10) buy entertainment.[4] Back in the 1940s, the poet T. S. Eliot saw this trend developing and worried that this would be the epitaph over modern man: "Here were a decent, godless people; Their only monument an asphalt road and a thousand lost golf balls."

Confusion. There are many people who go to your school, labor in your workplace, live in your neighborhood or occupy a place in your circle of friends or family who are searching for truth. Some of them believe in some concept of God, but they are confused. They are cobbling together a faith of sorts from the vast buffet of beliefs out there. They are buying books on spirituality or going to spiritually oriented websites. But merely being "spiritual" isn't going to give them what they most need. Like the Athenians to whom the apostle Paul spoke in Acts 17, many people today are swimming in information and have access to all kinds of knowledge. Yet too few possess the wisdom needed to change their character and relationships for the better. Many struggle to discern between the truly important versus the merely urgent matters of life.

The question is, will someone care enough to help them find the God who can guide them out of confusion and onto his way? Do people matter enough to you and me that we are willing to learn about their hopes and hungers, and start to describe the gospel and the way of God's kingdom in terms they can readily understand?

YEARN FOR PEOPLE TODAY

How do you regard the nondisciples within your reach? Do you have enough of God's passion for people to even *want* to be a witness to his heart for them? None of us is completely saturated with it. Our love is imperfect. Our knowledge of God is partial. Our confidence in being able to fulfill our calling is always something into which we are still growing. Here, however, are a few things you can do to evaluate your readiness to be a witness.

1. Check your motives. If you do not have a genuine love for people, a sense of how the gospel is truly good news and a humble willingness to learn more about how God might use you to help others get right with him, then you should probably stop right here. Go back and reread the first three chapters of this book and see if it fires up your passion further. If that still doesn't get it burning, put this book back on the shelf. Go read the daily news or *Discipleship Essentials* instead. Come back to this book when you feel an earnest desire to be used of God for his seeking and saving purposes.

If, however, you sense that, even though you have a long way to go, God has given you a longing to be a witness in a way that is very different from the experience had by the people interviewed on the Reno strip . . . if you are aware of how God's grace and truth have been good news to you . . . if you are open to stretching toward people in some new ways—then please keep reading.

2. Discern the needs of people near you. You may recall from our previous study

IT IS A SERIOUS THING TO LIVE IN A SOCIETY OF [ETERNAL BEINGS], TO REMEMBER THAT THE DULLEST AND MOST UNINTERESTING PERSON YOU TALK TO MAY ONE DAY BE A CREATURE WHICH, IF YOU SAW IT NOW, YOU WOULD BE STRONGLY TEMPTED TO WORSHIP, OR ELSE A HORROR AND A CORRUPTION SUCH AS YOU NOW MEET, IF AT ALL, ONLY IN A NIGHTMARE. ALL DAY LONG WE ARE, IN SOME DEGREE, HELPING EACH OTHER TO ONE OR ANOTHER OF THESE DESTINATIONS.

C. S. Lewis

(chap. 1) that Jesus called his disciples to be his witnesses first in Jerusalem and Judea (Acts 1:8)—the areas closest to them. There is a helpful principle here. Haddon Robinson observes:

A kind of arithmetic has been spawned in the counting rooms of hell. This kind of arithmetic is always interested in reaching the masses but somehow never gets down to a [particular] man or a woman. This kind of arithmetic always talks about winning the world for God but doesn't think much about winning a neighborhood for God. That arithmetic makes it valiant to cross oceans and never really crosses streets.[5]

Forget for a moment the charge to take the good news to the ends of the earth. Just think about what the gospel could mean to the people across your street, your school or workplace, your circle of friends or family. How might the message of Jesus seem like good news to these people at a point where they have already begun to recognize a need? As you reflect on the following questions, you may find it helpful to jot down some names in the margin.

- Who do you know who seems to be *injured at the core?* Maybe they appear to be driven by fear or anxiety, a sense of guilt, or simmering anger. Perhaps they've started to see this. Could this trouble have anything to do with an internal brokenness that only reunion with God can fully address? How might their life be better if God could heal and fill them at their center?

- Who in your circle of relationships seems *stuck in their character growth?* Maybe he or she has confessed an awareness of a lack of humility, peace or patience. Perhaps she or he struggles to be kind, good or faithful. Maybe gentleness or self-control seem painfully missing from this person's life. Would that person feel it to be a burden or a blessing to have a relationship with Someone who could change his or her character from the inside out?

- Who around you seems to be *hungering for guidance?* Has someone you know expressed a sense of feeling lost or unsure of what life is all about? Perhaps another person has talked about wishing he had a better-defined purpose for his days. Would these people benefit from having a clear vision of God's truth and a simple explanation of his plan for human life?

- Who do you know who is *aching over the problems of this world?* Maybe they

have spoken with you about particular people, needs or social issues that stir their heart. Would it hurt or help them to become part of a community of faith where they could link arms and gifts in bringing about some meaningful change in some important area?

- Who in your relational sphere is *feeling the weight of illness, death or grief* right now? Would it make any difference if there was someone (or a whole church) to stand with them in their pain? Could there come a time when it just felt natural to talk to such a person about a life that transcends the grave?

- Who around you is *longing for love?* Maybe she wishes someone loved her selflessly. Perhaps he wishes he knew how to love more fully and consistently. Would it help that person to be part of a community where loving one another and finding God's power to love more deeply was its very reason for being?

All of these people are in need of the gospel message.

3. Admit your own needs. As you went through the questions above, did you ever think: "I'm that person!" If so, that's good. The saving work of God takes a lifetime to exert its full influence upon even his most devoted followers. Every time we become aware again of how much we need the gospel, the better prepared we become to present it to others in the right spirit.

This realization also leads us to a further one. The experience of those casino-goers aside, it ought to be clear to us that the heart of Christian witness isn't the neurotic compulsion to throw something *at* people or to force something *into* people or to lay something *on* people. The heart of witness, Jesus-style, is the compassionate impulse to offer something good *for* people—something that addresses needs about which we, as well as the people we seek to reach, have at least begun to come to our senses (see Luke 15:17).

People can almost always tell when somebody is evangelizing them for the evangelizer's own sake. But they can also tell when someone is motivated by love and respect for them, attentive to their actual hopes and hungers, and convinced they have something helpful to offer; what such a Christian extends to them feels not like a gavel but a gift. They may or may not be ready to accept the gift at that particular moment, but Christian witness begins when someone meets a disciple who truly has the heart of the Gift-Giver.

4. Pray for God's power. Finally, to be this kind of agent of blessing, it is immensely important to go back to those original words of Jesus: "You will receive power when the Holy Spirit comes on you; and you will be my witnesses" (Acts 1:8). Jesus ties the effectiveness of his disciples' witness directly to the prevenient ("ahead-of-time") power of God's Holy Spirit. As

we'll explore further (chap. 6), the power of the Holy Spirit alone convicts people of their need of God and brings them to faith. We need God to act before our evangelistic actions can have great effect.

This is why there may be nothing so essential to your work as a witness as your willingness to pray. Popular evangelist Lee Strobel instructs us to be sure to "talk to God about people before talking to people about God." Ruth Bell Graham, wife of evangelist Billy Graham, quoting Tennyson, urged Christians to remember that "more things are wrought by prayer than this world ever dreams of." The apostle Paul, arguably the greatest missionary of all time, echoed these sentiments when he wrote: "Brothers and sisters, pray . . . that the message of the Lord may spread rapidly and be honored, just as it was with you" (2 Thessalonians 3:1 TNIV).

So pray to be filled with the yearning heart of God for others. Pray for the Holy Spirit's guidance in all your interactions with other people. Pray for God to do in others what only he can do to open them to his life. Pray in faithful confidence that, as you do, the power of God will move in such a way that someone precious to the great Seeker who is now lost will one day be found. What a celebration there will be in heaven when that day comes.

[1]Timothy Keller, *The Prodigal God: Recovering the Heart of the Christian Faith* (New York: Penguin, 2008).
[2]"Door Interview: Garrison Keillor," *The Wittenberg Door*, no. 82 (December/January 1985), p. 19.
[3]Arthur Miller, "The Bored and the Violent," *Harper's Magazine* 225, no. 1350 (November 1962): 51.
[4]Douglas Taylor-Weiss, Rector of St. Andrews Episcopal Church, Dayton, OH. See www.christianitytoday.com/ct/1997/march3/7t3049.html.
[5]Haddon Robinson, "A Case Study of a Mugging," *Preaching Today*, tape no. 102.

Application Exercise

1. What are the chief characteristics of the Pharisees and teachers of the law (Luke 15:2)?

2. How have you seen those characteristics in the Christian community today?

3. How do you think God feels toward those who are separated from him?

4. Jot down below the first name(s) of anyone you know who seems to exhibit one or more of the following characteristics:

☐ Injured at the core of his/her life:

☐ Stuck in his/her character growth:

☐ Hungering for guidance/truth:

☐ Aching over the problems of this world:

☐ Feeling the weight of illness, death or grief:

☐ Longing for true and eternal love:

5. How do you feel about people you know who don't yet know the gospel?

6. Complete this prayer: "Dear God, I know how deeply you love the people around me and yearn for them to know the blessings of the gospel. For this reason I ask you to . . ."

7. Does the reading convict, challenge or comfort you? Why?

Going Deeper

Keller, Tim. *The Prodigal God: Recovering the Heart of the Christian Faith*. New York: Penguin, 2008.

Kinnaman, David and Gabe Lyons. *unChristian: What a New Generation Really Thinks About Christianity . . . and Why It Matters*. Grand Rapids: Baker Books, 2007.

5 / Walk with People

LOOKING AHEAD

MEMORY VERSE: Luke 10:2
BIBLE STUDY: Mark 2:13-17
READING: Where the Action Is

 Core Truth

How do we begin to exercise our ministry as Christian witnesses?

Following Jesus, we move from our foundational communion with God into the mission field of an ill and injured world. Focusing on building redemptive relationships, we invest substantial time in people, express authentic affection for them, and gaze with both compassion and humility upon the damage done by sin to human health. These genuine friendships create the indispensable context for further influence.

1. Identify key words or phrases in the question and answer above, and state their meaning in your own words.

2. Restate the core truth in your own words.

3. What questions or issues does the core truth raise for you?

Memory Verse Study Guide

Copy the entire text here:

_____

_____

_____

_____

_____

_____

_____

_____

_____

_____

_____

_____

_____

_____

_____

_____

_____

_____

_____

Memory Verse: Luke 10:2

For many Christians, the spiritual life is thought of in terms of what happens in church, in our private devotional life, or in the context of how we manage our household. In this passage we look at where Jesus places his focus for the proclamation of the gospel message and the urgency he feels for this direction.

1. *Putting it in context: Read Luke 10:1-12.* Where does Jesus send the seventy-two disciples (v. 1)?

2. What do you think Jesus means when he says "the harvest is plentiful" (v. 2)?

3. What does Jesus tell his disciples to pray for and do and what might this have to say to his followers today (vv. 2-4)?

4. What particular blessings did Jesus ask his witnesses to bring to the people they met (vv. 5, 9)?

5. What was the basis on which his disciples were to judge whether to stay in or go from a particular place (vv. 5-12)?

6. What does this passage tell you about how Christ valued what his witnesses were offering to people?

7. How have these verses spoken to you?

Inductive Bible Study Guide

Bible Study: Mark 2:13-17

This study examines, once again, the contrast between the way that the religious leaders of Christ's day look at nonreligious people and the way that Jesus views them. It is set between several other narratives in which the Pharisees and teachers of the law find fault with what they perceive as a fundamental lack of "righteousness" on the part of Jesus, especially in his treatment of sick or sinning people.

1. *Read Mark 2:13-17.* What are the three different environments in which Jesus engages people in this brief passage (vv. 13-15)?

2. As you read the Gospels, do you get the impression that Jesus spent more time interacting with people inside the religious community or outside of it? What are the implications of that for you?

3. Even today, a lot of religiously oriented people spend as much time as possible with other religious people. Why would someone "eat with tax collectors and 'sinners'" instead (v. 16)?

4. In the NIV and some other translations, the word "sinners" is put in quotation marks when spoken by the Pharisees (v. 16) but not when Jesus uses it (v. 17). What might be the meaning of this?

5. How would you paraphrase in your own words Jesus' response to the Pharisees (v. 17)?

6. In what way are sin and sickness synonymous or related terms (v. 17)?

7. What questions or issues does this passage raise for you?

Reading: Where the Action Is

EVANGELISM VS. "EVANDALISM"

Now and then we hear of people who came to faith after a stranger accosted them on the street or at their doorway and asked them if they were sure about their eternal destiny. There are stories of people who became believers after they saw John 3:16 pasted on a placard someplace and then went home, read the text and found God using his Word to open up their heart.

More often than not, however, these rapid-fire forms of evangelism are experienced by people as a kind of "evandalism" rather than the gift of good news. People feel as if someone were throwing rocks or spraying paint at their soul. This random and perhaps shocking delivery of the gospel may seem desirable to Christians eager to rack up more evangelism points on their personal scorecard. It might appeal to those of us who feel too pressed for time to invest in a slower approach. But it does not often work well in an age where people have grown wary of Religion. More importantly, it is not the way of Jesus.

> THE MARK OF A GREAT CHURCH IS NOT ITS SEATING CAPACITY, BUT ITS SENDING CAPACITY.
>
> Mike Stachura

WHEN GOD WENT WALKING

God could have certainly settled for such a bulleted or blunt approach in reaching people. He could have simply written in the sky or stars: "Now is the moment of salvation. Turn from your sin. Believe in me and you shall be saved." As the apostle Paul points out in Romans 1, God arguably did reveal himself in the glory of Creation, but this was not sufficient to break through the blinded consciousness of most people. God could also have sent spectacular preachers to the planet—colorful communicators who would stand in the public square and shout out to people the error of their ways. This too was arguably tried in the person of the biblical prophets, with limited effect. So God, in his amazing love, did something more.

God's long walk. Eugene Peterson describes it like this: "The Word became flesh and blood, and moved into [our] neighborhood" (John 1:14 *The Message*). In other words, God made the long walk from the splendor and comfort of heaven to the comparative squalor and struggle of life on this earth. In the person of Jesus, he spent thirty years living in an ordinary family, working at a blue-collar job, and listening to the hurts, hopes and hassles of regular people. He then devoted most of the next three years to walking up and down the pathways of Palestine, looking for opportunities to meet people at their points of curiosity and need.

Beyond the steeple. It is obvious from reading the Gospels that some of Jesus' time was spent interacting with people inside the religious institutions of his day. The Bible describes Jesus sitting in the temple as a child, listening to the teachers there and asking them questions (Luke 2:46). We see him speaking in a local synagogue or teaching in the temple courts (Luke 4:16; 20:1). But far more often it was *out in the world* where Jesus conducted the ministry that so radically changed the lives of others. Instead of standing in a worship building, wondering why more people weren't coming in to find him there, God goes out to encounter people in the places where they live and work and play. We see Jesus conferring with people beside a lake or in someone's home, in the marketplace or on a hillside, along a bustling street or by a community watering hole (Mark 2:13, 15; Matthew 5:1-2; Luke 8:45; John 4:6).

Into everyday environments. Almost all of the illustrations Jesus used in his teaching were drawn from these everyday environments. He interpreted divine truth in terms of events, symbols and images with which nonreligious people would be familiar. His instruction was consistently aimed at helping people see how God meets them and wants to move through them in the course of day-to-day life. The Bible says that "the people were amazed at his teaching, because he taught them as one who

> THE TIME WHICH JESUS INVESTED IN THESE FEW DISCIPLES WAS SO MUCH MORE BY COMPARISON TO THAT GIVEN TO OTHERS THAT IT CAN ONLY BE REGARDED AS A DELIBERATE STRATEGY.
>
> Robert E. Coleman

had authority, not as the teachers of the law" (Mark 1:22). Jesus had the authority of someone who knew God and ordinary people unusually well. Out of this wellspring of relationship, Jesus prayed for people and wept with them. He said tough things few people wanted to listen to and tender things they desperately needed to hear. Jesus welcomed their questions and doubts about God. He was not deterred by their dirty feet, their soiled past or their inconsistent character. Summing up his intention to the people of the Old Testament, God had once declared: "I will walk among you and be your God, and you will be my people" (Leviticus 26:12). It was not until Jesus came, however, that anyone understood how personally committed God was to fulfilling this promise.

Focusing on a few. Jesus spent time with thousands of people. At the end of the day, however, he devoted an extraordinary amount of time to building a particularly deep relationship with twelve people, none of whom appear to have been very religious before he entered into conversation with them. He poured himself with even greater intensity into three of them—Peter, James and John. The result was that all of them became disciples of towering wisdom and strength. He gave his life *for* them, *to* them and *through* them, "leaving [us] an example," wrote Peter, "that [we] should follow in his steps" (1 Peter 2:21).

WALK WITH NEW EYES

If we are going to be Christ's witnesses, we need to follow his example very intentionally. Fewer and fewer nonbelievers today will spontaneously enter a church building or show up at a church-sponsored event. For this reason, the most fertile place for evangelism will be in Jesus-like encounters with people out where they are walking in the world.

> WHOEVER CLAIMS TO LIVE IN HIM MUST WALK AS JESUS DID. . . . HIS COMMAND IS THAT YOU WALK IN LOVE.
>
> 1 John 2:6; 2 John 1:6

As right as this sounds, however, actually gaining that orientation can be especially difficult if you are among the many of us whose focus of faith has traditionally been on what happens in and through traditional church structures. The institutional church has a very important role to play in equipping people for witness, but we must come to see it as only part of the larger context in which God aims for us to do our work. New eyes are needed.

1. See the church as your foundation. So long as it rests upon the Rock himself, the church remains a foundational part of God's plan. This truth is particularly vivid to me because I am blessed to be a member of an extraordinarily vital church. My best friends are here. My kids are nurtured here. Through the worship and growth ministries of the church, I and others encounter God and are equipped for life here. Because

the Bible is clear that we are to "do good to all, especially to those who are of the household of faith" (Galatians 6:10 TNIV), I know that one of my primary ministries is to love and care for people right here.

Whether your church is a cluster of four disciples meeting in a coffee shop, or ten in a home, or fifty in a college fellowship, or hundreds in a sanctuary or auditorium, you probably recognize how foundational to your life the Christian community is. Just don't let this *good* become the enemy of the *great.* The longer we are followers of Jesus and the better our church experience is, the easier it becomes for the bulk of our most important relationships to be those we have within the community of faith. After all, these people understand our faith and values. They like us or are like us. Church can become a very good comfort zone.

2. See the world as your mission field. Jesus knew that he had been sent not for the safety of the church but for the salvation of the world (John 3:16-17). He formed the church for the sake of reaching that larger mission field. The time Jesus spent investing in his disciples was partly so that they would have a foundational experience of the kind of loving communion he knew perfectly within the Trinity. Jesus wanted this love to be their strength as it was his (John 17). But the major reason he invested so deeply in his disciples was to ready them to go out and invest themselves in the lives of nondisciples who did not yet know the blessing of living within the communion of Father, Son and Holy Spirit (Matthew 28:18-20).

Other than the instructions he gave when he taught his disciples what we now call the Lord's Prayer (Luke 11:1-4)—a tremendously missional prayer in itself—there is only one occasion in the Gospels where we see Jesus telling his disciples what to pray for. "He told them, 'The harvest is plentiful, but the workers are few. Ask the Lord of the harvest, therefore, to send out workers into his harvest field'" (Luke 10:2).

Don't confuse your foundation (the church) with your mission field (those outside of the church). Don't let the good you experience in the life of the community of faith distract you from the Great Commission Christ has given all believers, including you. It's fine to pray for more people to come into our fellowships, but Jesus suggests that the bulk of our prayer ought to be for more of the church to go out walking, as he did, in the fields of this world.

The world is where the action is. It is out there where God wants to see new spiritual life birthed and new outposts of his kingdom established. The real measure of vitality for any church is not the number of people it gathers into a building for worship, but the number of people who go out from it as radiant witnesses to the heart of God for this world. "As the Father has sent me," says Jesus, "I am sending you" (John 20:21).

3. See people as your focus. Christ was always on the lookout for someone who was spiritually searching. Luke tells us that as Jesus was passing through Jericho (the financial market of his day), he spied a little man named Zacchaeus peering eagerly at him from up in a sycamore tree (Luke 19:1-5). John says that as Jesus was passing by the well at Sychar, he spotted a Samaritan woman coming down the road at midday (John 4:1-7). And Mark tells us that "as [Jesus] walked along, he saw Levi son of Alphaeus sitting at the tax collector's booth" (Mark 2:14).

Who will Jesus give you the power to see with fresh eyes as you go out this week? Maybe it will be the woman who works behind the counter or the parent you often see at the children's event. Perhaps it will be the fellow student or coworker you've passed a hundred times or the guy on the train. Maybe it will be a close friend, or a stranger in the waiting room. Ask Christ to give you his eyes for someone who may be struggling, searching and ready for someone to come alongside and walk with them.

BUILD REDEMPTIVE RELATIONSHIPS

We don't know how many times Jesus had passed Levi's tollbooth on his travels around Capernaum. We can't say for sure what Levi's issues were, although the fact that he was one of the despised class of tax collectors gives us a clue. Perhaps Levi had found that piling up money didn't bring him the joy he had expected. Maybe he found it hard to look in the mirror after living so long on the backs of other people. What we do know is that when Jesus finally said, "Follow me," Levi was ready to take a new step. "Levi got up and followed him" (Mark 2:14).

4. Spend time with people. When Levi began to follow Jesus, more than one option for educating this new disciple may have been available. For instance, Jesus could have escorted him to a local worship service or begun lecturing him on doctrine. But, instead, Jesus goes to Levi's house to enjoy a meal with him and a circle of his nonreligious friends. It is important to remember that meals in the first century were not dine-and-dash affairs. They were encounters in which people took off their shoes, lay around on cushions and lingered together over conversation for many hours. Mark says that "while Jesus was having dinner at Levi's house, many tax collectors and 'sinners' were eating with him and his disciples, for there were many who followed him" (Mark 2:15).

There was nothing sporadic or fleeting about Jesus' style of evangelism. He spent a lot of time with lost people. He spent what the Pharisees considered an ungodly amount of time with grungy fisherman, bartenders, political zealots and prostitutes. Strangely, all kinds of individuals who may generally have avoided religious people seemed to enjoy the company of Jesus. Why is this?

Could the reason be that Jesus was willing to hang out with them where *they* were comfortable, rather than trying to drag them into his comfort zone? Might it be that he talked with them about the things that interested *them?* Is it because Jesus never gave them the sense that they were projects, just genuinely important people to him? Could it be that Jesus was willing to take off his shoes, open his heart and lavish so much time on them? I suspect so.

Who are the people outside of the church that you are spending time with? If you don't know many people outside of your church or spend time with them, might it be time to invest in that pursuit? If you've invited non-Christians to church before and been frustrated by their negative response, could this be a sign that you need to get to know them—and let them know you better too—before asking them to leave their comfort zone?

5. Live carefully among people. There is

> EVANGELISM [MUST] MOVE FROM AN ACT OF RECRUITING OR CO-OPTING THOSE OUTSIDE THE CHURCH TO AN INVITATION OF COMPANIONSHIP. . . . THE CHURCH [MUST] WITNESS THAT ITS MEMBERS, LIKE OTHERS, HUNGER FOR THE HOPE THAT THERE IS A GOD WHO REIGNS IN LOVE AND INTENDS THE GOOD OF THE WHOLE EARTH.
> Darrell Guder

a stream of biblical teaching that reminds us to be careful as we engage people whose identity is rooted in the kingdom of this world rather than the kingdom of God. As a college student, I often extolled the virtues of "missionary dating" or "evangelistic partying." I believed that to have credibility and connection with people I needed to fraternize intensely with them. Looking back now, I know that I crossed the line of wisdom there on many occasions. Rather than being "salt and light" (Matthew 5:13-16) to people, I became absorbed in activities that did not advance God's good purposes in them or in me.

The apostle Paul cautions believers that "bad company corrupts good character" (1 Corinthians 15:33) and that there are times when to preserve our capacity for witness with worldly people we need to "come out from them and be separate" (2 Corinthians 6:17). The apostle James says that whoever wants to be a friend of the world makes himself an enemy of God (James 4:4). In his great prayer for the church, Jesus reminds his followers that "they are not of the world" (John 17:14).

At the same time, however, Jesus goes on to say to his Father, "My prayer is not that you take them out of the world but that you protect them from the evil one. . . . Sanctify them by the truth; your word is truth" (John 17:15, 17). Christ wants to make certain that our foundation in God's truth and fellowship is strong enough that we can enter the mission field with an identity and clarity against which the pull of the world does not prevail. But the vast weight of the New Testament makes clear that Jesus wants us out in that worldly field. He wants us to focus on building relationships of sufficient intimacy with people that he can do his redeeming work through us. As we'll see in coming chapters, it is out of these leisurely, long-lived relationships of authenticity and trust that there emerges the spiritual conversations God uses to draw people to himself.

6. Look on people with compassion. There are all kinds of people who never or rarely darken the door of a religious building for one of two reasons. The first reason is because they don't particularly like religious people. As we learned in chapter four, they find many people of faith to be uptight, controlling or critical. The second reason is because they've concluded that church people don't like them. They've learned that how they live, dress, make jokes or decorate their bodies sometimes makes people of faith very uncomfortable. If people feel judgment or criticism based on their outward appearance, they are unlikely to feel that their inner struggles will be viewed compassionately either.

Why are so many "Christians" unable to demonstrate and communicate affection for people who have struggles different than theirs or who are simply operating in logical consistency with their different worldview? Given the massive gap between the holiness of God and the remaining character and conduct defects in each of us, wouldn't you think that his extraordinary love toward us might just recondition our response to others (Romans 5:8)?

Martin Marty observes that one of the most significant problems for Christian witness today is that the people "who are good at being civil often lack strong convictions and the people who have strong convictions often lack civility," much less charity. [1] The simple truth of human nature, evidenced in the tax collectors' response to Jesus, is that people are always more eager to open their souls to someone who likes them than to someone who loathes them. Christians must become known as the ones most capable of looking at others through the lens of that amazing grace through which God gazes at us.

On hearing of the Pharisees' contempt for his interactions with sinners, Jesus said to them, "It is not the healthy who need a doctor, but the sick. I have not come to call the righteous, but sinners" (Mark 2:17). Jesus is saying that God looks at people not as deviants to be judged but as patients to be healed.

Suspend for a moment any polarizing associations you may have with the word *sin*. Just think for a moment about sin in terms of the struggles we each may have day by day with rage, lust, conceit, envy, anxiety, deceit, apathy or gluttony. Read today's news and notice where these impulses play a part in unfolding events. Imagine how the front page would alter if those impulses were replaced by what counteracts them: kindness, consideration, humility, generosity, peace, truthtelling, compassion and contentment.

Jesus once said that a human life can be thought of in terms of the dimensions of heart, mind, soul and strength (Luke 10:27). A healthy person is someone who is fed and fueled by love in all of these crucial dimensions. [2] Conversely:

- Consider the toll that rage, lust, conceit, envy, anxiety, deceit, apathy or gluttony takes on a person's bodily *strength*. Any physician can tell us how certain ingrained patterns of thought or behavior negatively affect one's circulatory, pulmonary, nervous and immune systems. It isn't merely alcohol, tobacco or French fries that destroy our bodies. The inner impulses that drive us to indulge in these things also can contribute to the degradation of our bodies.

- What happens to the health of our *mind* when it is filled with worries and obsessions and distorted ways of handling people and problems?

- When rage or conceit clogs someone's *heart*, why is it surprising that he or she boils over, or tramples others, or lacks the will to pursue the best?

- Sin erodes the health of our *soul* too: we can become fragmented, conflicted, disintegrated people, caught up in a culture that reflects these characteristics on a massive social scale.

The new message that Jesus brought was not the idea that God seeks to address this sin or to save sinners. Most Jews already got that. The remarkable news Jesus declared is that God loves people *while they are still sick with sin* (Romans 5:8). God's first response toward sinners is not condemnation but compassion. Those most mired in sin most need to meet this Christlike compassion in you.

7. Look with humility on people. Every bit as important as our compassion for lost sinners, however, is the crucial precondition for healing that Jesus' words in Mark 2 reveal: People must recognize for themselves that they are sick. For example, a person might consent to play golf with a doctor, or have polite conversation with her at a party, or even talk with the doctor's patients. But a person does not usually allow a doctor to perform an examination or prescribe medication unless they believe themselves to be sick.

The great British journalist Malcolm Muggeridge was once accosted by a skeptic who claimed that belief in God was just a crutch for the weak. With a twinkle in his eye, Muggeridge replied, "Ah, yes, but who of us isn't limping?" Who of us does not need the Great Physician? God views all of us as his patients (Romans 3:23; 6:23). Some of us, thankfully, have been under his care for a long time. Some people haven't yet accepted his care because they're afraid of the people in his hospital. Some don't even know that he is a doctor first and a judge second. Others have just been living with sickness and sick people for so long they don't realize what being healthy looks like—and they won't until they meet Jesus through God's Word or one of his witnesses.

Like Muggeridge, a true witness will be a humble one. It will never occur to him or her to say of someone, "How dare they do this or dress like that or say such things?" They see that this would be like saying to a sick person, "How dare your nose run?" No cancer survivor meets another patient—even one who may have brought the disease upon himself—and responds in a spirit of judgment. Instead, he or she is likely to be sympathetic and possibly say something like "I feel with you in your struggle. I pray that you find the best therapy. If you'd like me to share what's been helpful to me, just let me know."

FRIENDING VS. PHARISEEING

This is what makes the attitude of the Pharisees so appalling from Jesus' perspective. They don't seem to care at all about the ministry of healing. Imagine a soldier who kept running up to a medic on the battlefield, saying, "I was injured a little bit once but that got fixed. I haven't gotten shot or stepped on a landmine. I'm doing just fine. Why are you spending so much energy on these wounded people?" How long do you think it would be before the medic told you to get out of the way? No wonder Jesus was annoyed by the Pharisees.

Christ wants witnesses who are willing to come alongside the ill and the injured on life's battlefield and count it a privilege because they've been one of them. Harv Oostdyk, a legendary Young Life youth worker, was frequently asked by new coworkers what their strategy for evangelism should be. Oostdyk would simply smile and say: "Go out on the street and make some friends." We get a vivid picture of this kind of "friending" in the way that the biblical character Jonathan behaved toward David—a young man who at that point appeared to have a very uncertain future. If you study these passages on your own, you will see that Jonathan shows us how a true friend

- *attaches* himself to another, loving him as himself (1 Samuel 18:1-3; Proverbs 18:24)

- *affirms* the good and the gifts he sees in the other (1 Samuel 18:4-5)

- *admonishes* the other when he's in danger of further injury (1 Samuel 18:30—19:2)

- *advocates* for the other, advancing his best interests at each opportunity (1 Samuel 19:4-6)

- *aspires* for the other, seeking to help

him find strength in God (1 Samuel 23:16-18)

It was in no small way through the influence God gave to this friendship that David rose to become King of Israel. It was also through the friendship Jesus offered to that tax collector with whom he dined on that day long ago that Levi rose to become the apostle Matthew—the writer of the first Gospel. Who knows how the encouragement of a compassionate friend might impact the life of another?

Now it is your job to walk with people out in the world. Give thanks for your foundation in Christ, but always remember your mission field. Keep unfound people as your focus. Linger with them. Live carefully among them. Like them. Look upon their needs with compassion and humility. Build redemptive friendships with them. If you do this, you will be amazed at what God will do through you.

---

[1]Martin E. Marty, *By Way of Response* (Nashville: Abingdon, 1981), p. 81, as referenced in Richard Mouw, *Uncommon Decency: Christian Civility in an Uncivilized World,* rev. ed. (Downers Grove, IL: InterVarsity Press, 2010), p. 13.

[2]For a thorough exploration of this concept, see Greg Ogden, *The Essential Commandment* (Downers Grove, IL: InterVarsity Press, 2011).

➔ Application Exercise

1. How would you describe the practice of "evandalism"?

2. In which of the following areas do you have the greatest struggles and why?

   ☐ Lingering with people—spending significant time with them

   ☐ Living carefully among people—not getting dragged into bad behavior

   ☐ Loving people—feeling real humility before them and compassion toward them

3. Make a mark on the continuum below that represents where you sense you are right now in terms of your compassion and humility toward "sick" people.

   ├──────────┼──────────┼──────────┼──────────┼──────────┤

   I am like Jesus in my compassion   I am unlike Jesus in my compas-
   for sin-sick people.   sion for sin-sick people.

   ├──────────┼──────────┼──────────┼──────────┼──────────┤

   I feel profound humility because I   I need God to give me much
   know how sin-sick I am.   greater humility toward others.

4. On a scale of 1 to 4, rate yourself in terms of the following acts of befriending people

like those toward whom Jesus focused his energies.

(1 = Rarely; 2 = Occasionally; 3 = Frequently; 4 = Consistently)

_____ I attach my heart and time to such people, seeking to know them deeply.

_____ I affirm the good and the gifts I see in these people.

_____ I admonish (warn) people humbly about things I fear threaten them.

_____ I advocate for such people, trying to advance their best interests.

_____ I aspire for them to love God with heart, mind, soul and strength so they will grow in health and hope.

5. Write down below the names of two or three people with whom you sense God may be calling you to "walk" more intentionally in days ahead.

6. Take a moment now to pray for the people you identified above. Ask God to send you as a worker out into the field and to help you focus on deepening your relationship with them.

7. Does the reading convict, challenge or comfort you? Why?

Going Deeper

Hybels, Bill. *Just Walk Across the Room: Simple Steps Pointing People to Faith*. Grand Rapids: Zondervan, 2006.

6 / Investigate and Invest in the Soil

Looking Ahead

MEMORY VERSE: 1 Corinthians 3:6
BIBLE STUDY: Mark 4:1-20
READING: Spiritual Agriculture

 Core Truth

How can we further prepare ourselves and the people we walk with for significant spiritual influence?

To advance the work of witness, we must carefully investigate and invest in the spiritual soil of nondisciples' lives. Doing this requires clarity about who brings the harvest, an understanding of the types of ground on which the gospel seed is sown, and the loving boldness to ask the cultivating questions out of which life-changing spiritual conversations eventually arise.

1. Identify key words or phrases in the question and answer above, and state their meaning in your own words.

2. Restate the core truth in your own words.

3. What questions or issues does the core truth raise for you?

Memory Verse Study Guide

Copy the entire text here:

_____

_____

_____

_____

_____

_____

_____

_____

_____

_____

_____

_____

_____

_____

_____

_____

_____

_____

_____

Memory Verse: 1 Corinthians 3:6

In this brief verse, the apostle Paul sets forth several key aspects of the process by which the work of witness goes forward and bears fruit. It is helpful to know that Apollos was a Jewish convert to Christianity who was educated in Alexandria and an important Bible teacher at Ephesus and Corinth.

1. *Putting it in context:* This chapter of Paul's letter is aimed at addressing a particular problem among the Corinthian Christians. *Read 1 Corinthians 3:1-9.* What seems to be the issue that Paul seeks to set right?

2. What is "the seed" Paul is talking about, and in what way do you think he "planted it" (v. 6)?

3. What does Paul mean by saying, "Apollos watered it" (v. 6)?

4. Why does Paul stress that "God made it grow" (v. 6)?

5. How would you rank the relative importance of each of the persons who influenced the development of the church at Corinth and why?

Paul

Apollos

God

6. What does this verse teach you about the way faith develops in people?

7. How have these verses spoken to you?

Inductive Bible Study Guide

Bible Study: Mark 4:1-20

Jesus often told parables in which he described the spread of the gospel in agricultural terms (Matthew 13:24-30, 31-32; Mark 4:26-29). In the parable of the sower, Jesus communicates several insights that are important to the work of witness.

1. *Read Mark 4:1-8.* What are the four kinds of ground on which the farmer in Christ's parable sows his seed and what happens to the seed in each case?

   1.

   2.

   3.

   4.

2. Do you think it was wise or unwise for the farmer to sow the seed on so many different kinds of ground and why?

MANY PEOPLE TODAY ARE GETTING TIRED OF LIVING WITHOUT ULTIMATE PURPOSE: PUTTING IN HOURS AT THE OFFICE, PAYING THE BILLS AND MAKING ENDS MEET, KEEPING THEMSELVES ENTERTAINED WITH THINGS THAT RUST, FADE, AND WEAR OUT. MORE AND MORE ARE COMING TO THE POINT OF SAYING, "THERE'S GOT TO BE MORE TO LIFE THAN THIS!" AND HERE WE ARE, HOLDING THE KEYS TO MEANING IN THIS LIFE AND HOPE FOR THE NEXT. . . . WE NEED TO START SOME SPIRITUAL CONVERSATIONS AND FIND OUT WHO'S INTERESTED.

Bill Hybels and
Mark Mittelberg

3. *Read Mark 4:13-20.* Here Jesus unpacks the meaning of the parable of the sower for his curious disciples. He likens the different types of soil to the spiritual soil of people's lives. How would you describe the condition of each person he mentions?

   Person A:

   Person B:

   Person C:

   Person D:

4. On which of these kinds of people do you sense you ought to be focusing the majority of your efforts to sow the gospel seed and why?

5. *Read Mark 4:9-12.* Why do you think Jesus communicated his message in parables that made it difficult for people to understand his meaning?

6. What are the take-away messages from this passage for your work as a sower of the gospel seed?

7. What questions or issues does this passage raise for you?

Reading: Spiritual Agriculture

Sometimes Christians talk about evangelism as if it were a mechanical process. You say this, the other person says that, you respond this way. With the click of a mouse or the push of a button, others will be led to faith. It would be both convenient and in keeping with the pattern of today's technology-oriented culture if it worked this way. However, in his parables, as in his practice when interacting with people, Jesus likened the growth of the gospel in others to agricultural work rather than to mechanized processes.

REMEMBER WHO BRINGS THE HARVEST

Even when it is put in organic terms, the prospect of witnessing can feel like a burden. For some of us, it is a "positive burden." We are excited about the prospect of helping people come to faith. For others of us, this calling feels more like a "painful burden." We may feel up to the work of walking with people in love, but the thought of openly sharing our faith or leading others into the kingdom of God often feels like a daunting task.

> MOST PEOPLE WANT TO TALK ABOUT THINGS THAT REALLY MATTER—THEIR SENSE OF GOD, THEIR EXPERIENCES OF MEANING OR TRANSCENDENCE, THEIR ATTEMPTS TO COPE WITH THEIR OWN MORTALITY, THEIR STRUGGLES WITH GUILT AND GOODNESS, THEIR DREAMS AND HOPES AND DEEPEST LONGINGS. THEY WANT TO TALK ABOUT THESE THINGS BECAUSE, WITHOUT THEM, ALL THAT IS LEFT IN LIFE IS RE-RUNS AND SHOPPING, COPULATION AND DIGESTION, EARNING AND SPENDING AND SAVING, CULMINATING IN ESTATE SALES AND PROBATE.
>
> Brian McLaren

Human instrumentality. Whether positive or painful, this sense of burden comes from the feeling that the work of evangelism depends upon *our* action for its success, and on one level, it clearly does. Jesus told us that we were not only to be his disciples, but commissioned us to go and make disciples of all nations. He asked us to bring lost people home to the Father, Son and Holy Spirit. He charged us with responsibility to teach them to obey all that he has commanded us (Matthew 28:18-20). If the work of witness does not feel like a very weighty calling, then we haven't sufficiently thought about or embraced our mission.

Divine capacity. It is equally essential, however, to realize that the heaviest part of this mission rests not on our strength but on the person and power of God. To appreciate this, consider more closely the words with which Jesus introduces and concludes the commission he issues: "All authority in heaven and on earth has been given to me," says Jesus at the start of the commission. Then, at the other end of his famous charge, Jesus concludes, "Surely, I am with you always, to the very end of the age." What this means is that we can have confidence that Jesus holds all the power needed to accomplish everything in which he invites us to play a part. We can also trust that he is with us each and every step of the way till the mission is done. We do what we can, he does what we can't. Together we'll celebrate the results.

We and he. Randy Hurst calls this we-and-he interplay the "pattern of discipline and dependence."[1] We see this interplay when the apostle Paul encourages the Philippian Christians to "work out your own salvation with fear and trembling" but then adds, "for it is God who works in you to will and to act in order to fulfill his good purpose" (Philippians 2:12-13 TNIV). We see it again when Paul declares, "To this end I strenuously contend with all the energy Christ so powerfully works in me" (Colos-

THE KINGDOM OF HEAVEN IS LIKE A MUSTARD SEED, WHICH A MAN TOOK AND PLANTED IN HIS FIELD. THOUGH IT IS THE SMALLEST OF ALL YOUR SEEDS, YET WHEN IT GROWS, IT IS THE LARGEST OF GARDEN PLANTS AND BECOMES A TREE, SO THAT THE BIRDS OF THE AIR COME AND PERCH IN ITS BRANCHES.

Matthew 13:31-32

sians 1:29 TNIV). In both instances the apostle emphasizes the importance of our action (human instrumentality) and of God's (divine capacity).

Nowhere is this pattern more vividly seen than in the work of Christian witness. You and I are asked to be disciplined instruments in God's effort to help others find new life in Christ, but we depend on God's capacity to supply the spiritual power that actually renews people. The Bible teaches that the Holy Spirit alone "will convict the world of guilt in regard to sin and righteousness and judgment" (John 16:8). Only the Spirit of God can guide people "into all truth" (John 16:13). Jesus often stressed this reality in the parables he told about the sowing of seed. "This is what the kingdom of God is like," he once said. "A man scatters seed on the ground. Night and day, whether he sleeps or gets up, the seed sprouts and grows, though he does not know how. All by itself the soil produces grain—first the stalk, then the head, then the full kernel in the head. As soon as the grain is ripe, he puts the sickle to it, because the harvest has come" (Mark 4:26-29).

Do you see the pattern here? The man in Christ's story is responsible for sowing the seed, but it is not by his power that the seed grows. Whether he dozes or hovers over the seed, he can't affect the speed of growth. He can only sow, perhaps water the ground a bit, and then wait for the power within the seed to do its work. The apostle Paul understood this interplay clearly. In his letter to the church at Corinth, Paul wrote: "What, after all, is Apollos? And what is Paul? Only servants, through whom you came to believe—as the Lord has assigned to each his task. I planted the seed, Apollos watered it, but God has been making it grow. So neither he who plants nor he who waters is anything, but only God, who makes things grow. . . . For we are God's co-workers" (1 Corinthians 3:5-9 TNIV).

Trust and obey. Remember this the next time you become anxious at the thought of leading someone to Christ. Sowing the seed of the gospel and watering it where you can is *your* work as a witness. When and how that seed sprouts or bears fruit in someone's life, however, is the work of *God*. God alone brings the harvest. It takes many planters, waterers and the unseen action of God to bring the harvest to bloom in someone. You may or may not get to see "the full kernel in the head" (Mark 4:28). So don't measure your success as a witness by how much of the harvest you see. Gauge your performance by how faithfully you have sown the seed where the Spirit led.

SURVEY THE SOIL

If we want to cooperate with God in help-ing people toward conversion then it is also crucial that we understand something about the various kinds of soil in which the seed of the gospel is sown. In his famous parable of the sower (Mark 4:1-20), Jesus said that people's hearts are like soil whose basic condition will profoundly affect their ability to accept the gospel message at the time we may seek to sow it.

Ravaged ground (v. 15). Some people, said Jesus, are like ground under attack by birds. You may faithfully share the gospel message with them, but God's enemy (Satan) comes and "takes away the word" before it has the chance to take root. I think of a student with whom I often talked about spiritual matters, but who was so regularly influenced by a group of friends hostile to God that the good I sowed there seemed just as quickly attacked and devoured by them. Every encounter I had with this person seemed to involve starting all over again.

Rocky ground (vv. 16-17). Other people you meet, says Jesus, will be like rocky places. For a moment, they may seem receptive to the gospel message. They may enter into the spiritual discussion with apparent fascination or joy. Yet beneath the surface is very hard ground. They've lived for such a long time with a heart hardened against a true, responsive relationship with God that the seed of the gospel fails to take root. Many of us see this at holiday times or following a season of crisis. People pour into churches at Christmas or Easter in staggering numbers. In seasons of public disaster or personal pain, people will suddenly seem very open to what God has to say to them. For a moment, they are alive to faith. When they discover, however, that this newfound connection doesn't prevent trouble or persecution, "they quickly fall away." The ground of their heart wasn't truly ready to accept the seed at the deep level needed.

Reluctant ground (vv. 18-19). Then there are those people, said Jesus, whose lives are so congested with "the worries of this life, the deceitfulness of wealth and the desire for other things" that these things, like weeds in an overrun garden, choke off whatever spiritual seed is planted in them. I met a man at a cocktail party who had many spiritual questions. Conversation with him there led to an ongoing discussion between us. A crisis with one of his kids made him even more interested in exploring deep matters of faith and life. In time, he joined a small group Bible study with me. But his interests were divided. He derived great pleasure from spending money, running his business and conducting his relationships according to his own rules. As the very different way God wanted him to manage these affairs became clearer, he was reluctant to give God control. Eventually, the thorns of these other allegiances choked out his desire for God and he became terribly lost once again, ending up going to prison for white-collar crime.

Ready ground (v. 20). The good news is there will also be people whose hearts are like "good soil." The ground of their lives will have been well tended. Their hearts will be soft and their minds open enough to really receive at a deeper level the seed of the gospel message. Maybe they understand how badly they need to get right with God or need his power to overcome their character flaws. Perhaps they see how much they need to set their life's course by his reliable truth; perhaps they long to participate in his redemptive work in this world. Maybe they want the absolute assurance he offers that they can enjoy life beyond the grave or can be filled with the greatest love of all. When they hear the gospel, they "hear the word, accept it, and produce a crop—thirty, sixty or even a hundred times what was sown."

I think of Vincent, a tough businessman with a drinking problem and a marriage on the rocks. Many fine witnesses had tried to sow into his life over the decades. They met him at points when the soil of his life was full of rocks or weeds, or besieged by the enemy. By God's grace, I got to be there when that soil was well prepared. There began a three-year period in which Vincent, a small group of others and I explored the deep things of God and life. I watched in amazement as God led Vince into a recovery program for his addiction and a counseling ministry for his marriage.

Jesus once said that the kingdom of God was like a tiny mustard seed which, if planted on good soil, could become a tree so large it would provide shelter for many (Matthew 13:31-32). I saw that slow-growing miracle in Vincent's life. Today, he is one of the most dedicated Christian disciples I know. He leads his business and seeds a variety of kingdom-building ministries with integrity, wisdom and generosity. His winsome witness continues to help many nondisciples find their way into the family of God. What a magnificent harvest has come from the tiny seed sown in the open soil of this one man's life.

Respect the ground. Sometimes it will be very obvious what kind of spiritual soil you are dealing with as you walk with the nondisciples around you. If you are meeting nothing but hard-baked ground, don't devote all your time sowing seed there. There are ways of dropping a verbal seed or two that we'll discuss in chapter seven. There are other ways of witnessing to unready people that we'll also explore in depth in chapters eight through ten. But don't spend all your seed-sowing energy on someone who clearly does not have "ears to hear" at that moment (Mark 4:9). This is why Jesus spoke in parables. He scattered a bit of provocative truth on people and then waited to see who was spiritually *ready* enough to come and ask him for more.

Most people's lives are mixed ground. There is some part of them that is under attack, some part open but still rocky, some part reluctant to abandon the thorny sources of life that choke the gospel seed.

> BE WISE IN THE WAY YOU ACT TOWARD OUTSIDERS; MAKE THE MOST OF EVERY OPPORTUNITY. LET YOUR CONVERSATION BE ALWAYS FULL OF GRACE, SEASONED WITH SALT, SO THAT YOU MAY KNOW HOW TO ANSWER EVERYONE.
>
> Colossians 4:5-6

But if we study their soil carefully, we will find some time or place where they are ready for new life. We just need a vision for how to engage them in that place.

ASK CULTIVATING QUESTIONS

My wife, Amy, is a wonderful gardener. She spent part of her youth in rural Mississippi working in the fields, participating in 4-H clubs, learning how things grow. To this day she can look at a plot in our yard and discern what is going on with that soil. What looks like dirt to me is to Amy's eye a field of opportunity. She can see how much sand or clay is there and what kind of amendment to the soil is needed to make it more fertile. She can spot amidst a tangle of greenery the weeds or parasites that need removing or the excess that needs pruning. Amy knows what new seeds might grow well.

Spiritual farming is like this. We need to have so investigated the ground of people's lives that we know where and how to invest our energies. One of the most effective ways of gaining this intimate access is to start asking people "cultivating questions." They are *cultivating* in that they help you get under the surface of the soil and start to turn up places of need and opportunity where God and you can invest. Try the following five *entry point*s with people.

1. Investigate longings for greater life. The Bible teaches that God "has planted eternity in the human heart" (Ecclesiastes 3:11 NLT). He has made each human being in his image and likeness (Genesis 1:26) and left an impress of his life upon people that has been corrupted but never completely eradicated by sin. What this means is that whether someone is self-consciously "spiritual," a hardened atheist, a self-satisfied agnostic or a convicted criminal, every person you meet has within them a vestigial longing for the very things for which God has made us.

Down deep in the soil of everyone's life are five essential longings, planted there by God: (1) to love and be loved, (2) to grow in grace and wisdom, (3) to give a gift that matters to others, (4) to sow a seed that leaves a legacy, and (5) to sing a song of joy instead of marching to life as a dirge. For many years my practice has been to describe these longings to nondisciples and then ask if they can identify with any of them. Everyone can. Some people are not very interested in talking about religion, especially if they do not know you very well. Almost everyone, however, will be open to talking about their longings. They may not use the exact words supplied above to describe what they yearn for but, if you inquire, you will find echoes of these impulses in everyone.

I have found the following questions to be helpful when engaging nondisciples with the gospel:

- What do you long for in life?

- What do you wish could be different, deeper or better in your life?

- What really brings a smile to your face or a thump to your heart?

- What are some values and virtues you want to pass on to your kids?

- What do you hope people will say about you when you die?

- Where do you get the perspective or the power to live the life that you have envisioned for yourself amidst all that distracts and deters you?

It's important to show a profound interest in and respect for the yearnings that people express, because they are the cry of the God-shaped vacuum in people's hearts. Let them know that you have longings like these too and that you are finding answers to them. Don't insist on telling where you've found these answers yet, unless they specifically ask. Your mission at this stage of the conversation is to demonstrate that when it comes to the deepest hopes about life, the soil of your soul is a lot like theirs. Be patient.

2. Investigate tainted earth. I've learned from my wife that some ground doesn't produce fruit because it is tainted in some way. It may have been exposed to chemicals that make it inhospitable to the growth of plant life. This can be true with spiritual growth too. Some of the people around you have not become disciples because something has contaminated their soil. They've seen bad examples of faith. They've heard distorted teaching or think of God only in negative terms. They may have understandable worries or uncertainty about what following Jesus would mean.

Get your hands into that dirt and find out what has poisoned it to the growth of the gospel in them. Ask people questions like these:

- What are your impressions of God?

- What have been your experiences of Christians or the church?

- What has made it hard to think seriously about pursuing Christianity further?

- What do you feel you'd lose if you became a follower of Jesus?

- If you could ask one question of God, what would it be?

Try to understand what may be blocking their spiritual growth and show them that you care about them.

When talking with people about these kinds of deep, personal issues, be wary of rushing to argue with what people may share. Simply seek to understand the character of the soil. If they are willing to risk revealing their questions or hurts to you, demonstrate that they can trust you. Show them how seriously you take their concerns. Asking questions that invite them to tell you more about their experiences, questions and difficulties may help them to open up. Specific questions and responses that can be helpful include

- Tell me more about that.

- What was that like?

- I can see why you might feel that.

- That would have been very hard or upsetting to me too.

- Thank you for letting me inside of that.

Don't try to solve or salve things for people at this point. Just show them that you are willing to share in the complexity of this soil. Again, just be in the dirt with them.

3. Investigate shading issues. Some years ago, following a violent storm, we were required to cut down a very tall pine tree in our backyard. Soon after the pine tree was removed our small pear tree began a process of dramatic and unexpected growth. Suddenly out from beneath the shade of the dominating pine, the little tree grew up toward the light. Some of the people you know are not growing toward Christ because they sit beneath a similarly oppressive shade. In their case, this shadow may be created by questions with difficult answers. Until we cut down this problem and expose them to more light they may not grow much further in their faith.

Before I came to faith I had plenty of questions myself. Some of the questions I asked were frivolous (like, Why are there so many Christian denominations?). I didn't really care about the answers. The questions were just a way to avoid more serious spiritual engagement. Other questions I asked were aimed at putting Christians on the defensive, like the question Pilate posed to Jesus: "What is truth?" (John 18:38). The reality was that I, like Pilate, would not have accepted any answer that limited my lifestyle at that time.

Some of my questions, however, were earnest ones, such as, Why should I believe in God? What's to say that the Bible is different than any other book? How can Jesus be the only way to heaven? Why do bad things happen to good people and good things to wicked ones? Getting answers to these questions wasn't what brought me to faith, but the fact that there were some Christian disciples who took these queries seriously, didn't seem surprised or scared by them, and offered me some kind of thoughtful response removed some of the "shadowing pines" that were blocking me from growing further.

I bet this is true too for some of you reading this book. It is definitely true for some of the nondisciples you know. So find out what their earnest issues are. Ask them what intellectual obstacles may be keeping them from Christian belief. At the beginning of your dialogue don't worry so much about having all the answers. Feel free to tell them if you don't know the answer to a question they ask, and let them know that you will try to find information that will help you both work through the question. Don't offer pat answers or feel as though all loose ends must be tied up in one sitting. Simply being someone whom nondisciples know genuinely cares about their questions may be sufficient to begin restoring damaged or unreceptive soil. Pray for God to grow this capacity in you. You may be surprised by the growth that occurs in this light.

4. Investigate parasites and blight. Along the way, it is also helpful to investigate what may be eating away at the health of or stunting the greater life for which the questioning people you know sincerely long. Unless you know the person fairly well, it is likely unwise to *start* your inquiry here, lest their discomfort in talking about the problem areas of their life shut down the conversation prematurely. As we'll explore further when we get to chapters seven and eight, this kind of dialogue will be much more natural after you've demonstrated the ability to go to these vulnerable places yourself.

If a person begins to open his or her heart to you by sharing fears or failings, you probably have the trust needed for this kind of deeper investigation. At this point, dare to ask people these kinds of questions: Are there any ways in which you feel that your life hasn't turned out like you hoped it would? What do you feel blocks you from having the life you want? Is there a flaw in your character that particularly hurts or haunts you? Do you think it is possible for that limit ever to be overcome? Why or how?

In these moments you have a wonderful opportunity to love people as Jesus loves them and help them with difficult feelings and issues. If you have built the confidence needed for this kind of conversation, you will also find that nothing so moves a relationship to a more spiritually fertile place as getting a shared understanding of the parasites or blight that someone senses has limited his or her life.

5. Investigate traces of the gardener. Finally, see what you can discover about the "traces of God" already evident in the soil of nondisciples' lives.[2] If a truly loving God exists, as Christians maintain, then you would expect to find traces of his gracious hand at work in the lives of people, whether they acknowledged him by name or not (Matthew 5:43-45).

It is just this kind of evidence that became the fascination of Harvard psychiatrist M. Scott Peck, as detailed in his famous book, *The Road Less Traveled*. While not a Christian at the time, Peck found himself increasingly impressed by a remarkable pattern in the experience of the people he studied, irreligious and not. Hundreds of people were telling vivid stories of having experienced a mysterious and benevolent power at work on the personal level. They described a conviction that some unseen hand had orchestrated remarkable conversions of circumstances that worked for their good. They spoke of a benevolent Presence coming alongside them in moments of tremendous distress. They told of being supplied from beyond themselves with seemingly impossible insight or sudden strength. The common theme in the working of this power was that it served to nurture—support, protect and enhance—human life.[3] Ultimately, the weight of this research, a further study of experiences of "evil," and the discovery of a stunning correspondence between these phenomena and the witness of the Bible, were overwhelming to Peck. He became a convert to the Christian faith.

Who do you know that might be able to describe personal encounters with the Gardener's gracious hand, even if he or she has not yet recognized his name? Ask people if they have ever experienced an alignment of providential circumstances that seemed to defy probability, or if they have ever felt a comforting Presence coming alongside them in moments of need or wonder, or if they have ever been supplied with a wisdom or power that seemed not their own. The answer may be no. But it may be yes. If you get the latter response from even one person, think of the discussion that might unfold.

Consider the Ultimate Fruit

Investigating the spiritual soil of people's lives can change for the better the nature of your connection with them. It can open up dialogue about more explicit issues of faith and life. It can help prepare the ground for that day when you have the chance to testify yourself to how Christ and his gospel have met you at your greatest points of longing and need of grace. If you think that making this kind of investigation could be a time-consuming and strenuous effort, you are correct. The secret to developing the perseverance needed, however, lies in considering the ultimate outcome.

When U.S. president James Garfield was principal of Hiram College in Ohio, a man approached him quite irritated by his son's slow progress through school. The father asked if the course of studies might be shortened so that his son could complete his degree in less time. "Why, certainly" Garfield replied. "But it all depends on what you want to make of your boy. When God wants to make an oak tree he takes a hundred years. When he wants to make a squash, he requires only two months. Tell me, sir, which fruit did you have in mind?"

There is no Miracle-Gro to speed up progress in the spiritual life. There is only the hoping heart, the wise mind and the persevering hand of the Gardener. But if you will trust the Lord of the harvest, survey the soil and ask plenty of cultivating questions, you will find that this is more than enough to further the process by which great fruitfulness comes.

[1]Randy Hurst, *Response Evangelism: Ready to Reach When God Gives Opportunity* (n.p.: Access Publishing, 2008), p. 17.

[2]Diogenes Allen, *Traces of God* (New York: Church Publishing, 2006).

[3]M. Scott Peck, *The Road Less Traveled: A New Psychology of Love, Traditional Values and Spiritual Growth* (New York: Touchstone Books, 1998), p. 260.

Application Exercise

1. In your own words, describe the relationship between human instrumentality (discipline) and divine capacity (dependence) in the work of evangelism?

2. Take a few moments to read through the conversion stories described in the Scripture passages below. Which of these experiences most closely resembles your own journey? Take some time to reflect on this and write down some of the ways these experiences are similar to and different from your own.

   ☐ A decisive *alteration* from one spiritual path to Christ's higher one (the Ethiopian eunuch, Acts 8:26-39; Cornelius, Acts 10)

   ☐ A sudden *reversal* of orientation from disbelief/nondiscipleship to faith/followership (Zacchaeus, Luke 19:1-10)

   ☐ A gradual *transformation* of perspective from religiosity to relationship with God (the apostle Paul, Acts 9:1-30)

3. Draw a line between the basic longings described on the left and any of those dimensions of the gospel message listed on the right that may address these yearnings. How might understanding these connections be helpful as you relate to nondisciples?

To love and be loved	**G**et right with God
To grow in grace and wisdom	**O**vercome your character flaws
To give a gift that matters	**S**et your course by reliable truth
To sow a seed that continues	**P**articipate in kingdom change
To sing a song of joy	**E**njoy life beyond the grave
	Love with the greatest love of all

4. Write down three questions that strike you as particularly helpful in your future efforts to investigate the spiritual soil of people's lives.

5. Write the names of two or three people to whom you feel led to ask these questions. Next to their names, jot down an adjective to describe what you sense is the condition of their soil at present (ravaged, rocky, reluctant, ready).

6. As you consider people you've identified above, write down what factors lead you to these conclusions about their readiness to respond to the gospel. In what specific ways can you demonstrate your interest in their lives?

7. Does the reading convict, challenge or comfort you? Why?

Going Deeper

Pippert, Rebecca Manley. *Out of the Saltshaker and Into the World: Evangelism as a Way of Life*. Downers Grove, IL: InterVarsity Press, 1999.

Part Three

DISPLAYING CHRIST IN YOU

St. Francis of Assisi is often quoted as saying, "Preach the gospel at all times. If necessary, use words." In this exhortation is a dependable truth: Christianity is more easily caught than it is taught. This is not to say that there's no place for verbal teaching. As we learned in chapter two, and will explore further in chapter eleven, it is essential that every disciple have a solid understanding of the gospel message and be able to explain it clearly. Having said this, however, the message we proclaim will have much greater credibility if it is housed within a whole life whose witness demonstrates the words we utter. This section focuses on what it looks like to display the life-changing power of Christ.

Testify to the Truth You Know (chap. 7). We begin by examining a part of your witness where using words is absolutely necessary. Each of us is called to testify to the truth we know about God, life and self in a manner that helps renew the thoughts and feelings other people have about Christ and the Christian faith. We'll look at what goes into each of the three principal types of testimony and how you can equip yourself to practice them in a gentle, respectful and influential way.

Nail the Sins That Slay You (chap. 8). Next, we'll take a hard look at the ineffective way some witnesses deal with their own character flaws and those of others, and what Jesus has to say about this. Few things limit the credibility of our witness more than untransformed Christians can. You'll identify some specific steps you can take to avoid being among that number. You'll also catch a glimpse of what it looks like to be a disciple who names and addresses their own character issues in a manner that makes others who wrestle with their own need for change want to approach you rather than avoid you.

Express Grace Under Pressure (chap. 9). Nothing so reveals what a person is truly made of as how they behave under pressure. In this chapter we'll explore some of the most common circumstances where significant pressure comes upon a witness's life. You'll see how you can respond to such trials in your own life in way that reveals the power of God at work within you. Far from being occasions to be hidden or escaped from, these moments can actually become your finest hours as a witness.

Serve Needs (chap. 10). Finally, we'll consider the enormously influential role that taking the form of a servant has in Christian witness. As disciples, we follow a Lord who exerted his greatest power not by pursuing comfort or privilege, but by meeting people at the point of their messiest needs. You'll identify some particular ways that you can display the love of Christ and encourage in others a desire to get closer to him.

7 / Testify to the Truth You Know

LOOKING AHEAD

MEMORY VERSE: 1 Peter 3:15
BIBLE STUDY: John 9:1-34
READING: Your Courtroom Witness

 Core Truth

What testimony can we offer to help people move toward a positive verdict on the gospel?

We can help renew the thoughts and feelings of people toward Christ and Christianity by testifying to the truth we know through three major types of testimony: a prosecutorial style that respectfully confronts people with tough questions; a defensive style that supplies reasoned answers to intellectual barriers to faith; and a personal style which gently leads people into the story of God's work of grace in our life.

1. Identify key words or phrases in the question and answer above, and state their meaning in your own words.

2. Restate the core truth in your own words.

3. What questions or issues does the core truth raise for you?

Memory Verse Study Guide

Copy the entire text here:

——————————————

——————————————

——————————————

——————————————

——————————————

——————————————

——————————————

——————————————

——————————————

——————————————

——————————————

——————————————

——————————————

——————————————

——————————————

——————————————

——————————————

——————————————

——————————————

——————————————

Memory Verse: 1 Peter 3:15

The apostle Peter makes clear that a very significant part of a disciple's witness is testifying to the truth they know. In this verse, he helps us see some essential dimensions of this ministry.

1. *Putting it in context:* Peter's words are offered at the close of a letter to the church at a time when it was under attack from a skeptical world and in danger of being absorbed by it. He urges disciples to retain their holy distinctiveness in all their relationships, and especially in the way they conduct themselves with nonbelievers.

   Read 1 Peter 3:8-16 and Matthew 5:13-16. What common themes are expressed in these two passages?

2. Why is "setting apart" or "revering" Christ as Lord relevant to this vision (1 Peter 3:15)?

3. When and for what are disciples supposed to be prepared?

4. What do you think it means in this context to "always be prepared"?

5. Peter suggests that witness should come in response to people "asking" about our hope. How does this differ from other notions of evangelistic witness?

6. Very briefly, what is "the reason for the hope that you have"?

7. What are the two specific qualities Peter says that witnesses are supposed to bring to their testimony in verse 15?

8. What additional quality of a witness's life does Peter highlight in verse 16?

Inductive Bible Study Guide

Bible Study: John 9:1-34

The story of the blind man (some refer to him as Bartimaeus—see Mark 10:48) offers us a wonderful window into many dimensions of Christian witness in any age. We get a vivid picture of the manner of Christ's gracious work in a person's life. We hear how one man bears personal testimony to the good God has done in him. We see how the disciples and Pharisees alike struggle to understand the heart God has for people. And we get a glimpse of the resistance some people have to accepting the truth about God.

1. How is being "blind from birth" a helpful metaphor for the condition from which human beings need a cure (v. 1)?

2. Christ's disciples held a belief, common in ancient times, that a person's physical maladies were the result of his own sins or that of earlier generations (vv. 1, 34). What does Christ's answer suggest about where God puts his emphasis when he looks at needy people (vv. 3-5)?

> IN THE MIDST OF A
> GENERATION SCREAMING
> FOR ANSWERS, CHRISTIANS
> ARE STUTTERING.
>
> Howard Hendricks

3. Jesus smears mud on the blind man's eyes and tells him to "go . . . wash in the Pool of Siloam." The man accepts this treatment, follows Christ's instructions and "came home seeing" (vv. 6-7). What does this progression suggest to you about the process of God's saving work?

4. The man's neighbors are amazed by his healing and want to know more about how it happened (vv. 8-10). The man, however, simply tells his story (v. 11). This catalyzes further questions as the neighbors now want to learn how they can find the One who performed this miracle (v. 12). What does this tell you about the effect that a witness's testimony can have?

5. In contrast to the neighbors' reaction, note the response of the Pharisees to this miracle of grace (vv. 13-16, 26-29, 34). In what ways is this like the response that some nondisciples in our day have to our claims that Christ is the Savior?

6. The blind man's parents are intimidated by the authority of the Pharisees (vv. 18-23). How is their response similar to the one that some believers have to the skeptics in our time?

7. The healed man attributes his recovery to the supernatural grace of God at work through Jesus in his life and tries to defend his convictions through rational argument (vv. 13-18). When the skeptics won't hear of that, he offers one clear statement (v. 25) and leaves it at that. Why is this form of testimony powerful?

Reading: Your Courtroom Witness

CHRISTIANITY ON TRIAL

Christianity is on trial today, no less than when Jesus stood before Pilate and Herod in the first century long ago. Many of the people we know are trying to make up their minds about Christ and his Way. One of our most important roles as witnesses is to provide testimony that helps them come to a positive verdict. It was said of John the Baptist, "He came as a *witness* to *testify* concerning that light [Christ], so that through him all might believe" (John 1:7 TNIV, italics mine). The apostle John later wrote, "The life appeared; we have seen it and *testify* to it" (1 John 1:2, italics mine). Christ uses the *testimony*—that is, the verbal or written witness—of his disciples to help draw people to him.

Paul taught that spiritual transformation happens for people through the "renewing of [the] mind" (Romans 12:2). By "mind" Paul meant both thoughts and feelings.[1] The stereotypes people hold, the intellectual propositions they rely on, the attitudes they have about matters of belief, are always a mixture of thoughts and feelings. Conversion involves changing this "mind," and our testimony can help to catalyze this process of renewal.

Think about the courtroom context again. The members of a jury form an opinion about the merits of a case largely on the basis of *three kinds of testimony*. They listen to the prosecuting attorney, to the defense attorney and to the persons on the stand. While the judicial metaphor has to be seasoned with much grace, let's review it as a means of exploring some crucial aspects of a witness's testimony.

> THE LOVELY PART OF BEING A WITNESS IS THAT YOU CAN'T COMPEL BELIEF. ALL YOU CAN DO IS SAY: HERE IS WHAT HAPPENED. IN SAYING THIS THE WITNESS IS ONLY DOING HIS JOB; HOW PEOPLE RESPOND IS THEIR OWN BURDEN, THEIR OWN RESPONSIBILITY. WHOM WOULD YOU SAY HAS MORE CREDIBILITY: THE MAN WHO POUNDS ON THE TABLE INSISTING HIS STORY IS TRUE, OR THE ONE WHO, HAVING THE REPUTATION OF HONESTY, FREES HIS LISTENERS TO DECIDE FOR THEMSELVES?
>
> Leif Enger

PROSECUTORIAL TESTIMONY

At my family's table sit two federal prosecutors, three law school professors, and two U.S. Supreme Court clerks. It is not always comfortable to be in the presence of minds like this. My relatives often ask me pointed questions that require careful thought about what I believe and why I believe it. Because they love me, have listened to me and have walked with me for a long time, I know that when they press me it is not for self-interested reasons. They want to improve my mind and help me find truth. Some of the people you know need an advocate like this when it comes to their thoughts and feelings on matters of faith.

Be willing to ask tough questions. A few years ago I met a nondisciple who shared with me that he'd grown up in a harsh, legalistic Christian home. On several occasions, Gary stressed that this was the reason why he was no longer interested in Christianity. For a long time, I just tried to resonate with how difficult his childhood must have been. One day, however, I felt led to press the matter a bit further. I recounted my own experience of growing up under the care of a dentist who physically abused me. For years, it made me avoid dentists altogether. When I related the story to Gary, I said, "One day the truth hit me. That man was a very bad dentist. But these are *my* teeth. Am I going to go my whole life bypassing the benefits of dentistry because that particular doc was a quack?" There was a moment of quiet at the table. "Gary," I said, "I like you a lot, so let me dare to ask you a difficult question. How long are you going to let the bad experience you had with certain Christians stop you from getting proper care for your soul? What if there are actually some great spiritual doctors out there?" Gary is now a regular at our church—not a believer yet, but he's seeking again.

Prosecutorial testimony requires loving people enough to ask questions that may seem tougher than the ones we reviewed in the last chapter. For example:

- How would you describe your spiritual condition?

- What have you done to nourish your spiritual life?

- What are the sources you've consulted to examine the evidence for God, the divinity of Jesus or the authority of the Bible?

- What will you say to God if it turns out he exists and that Jesus was indeed the lifeboat he sent you?

- If you became a follower of Jesus as the Son of God and it turned out he wasn't, would you have lost more or less than if you didn't follow him and it turned out he was?

- If heaven exists, on what basis will you be welcomed there?

Have clear, solid answers. Spiritual prosecutors confront people with tough questions. They don't make these queries in a condemning, critical or superior spirit, as if to say, "I have all the right answers and you obviously don't." But they do have answers to the questions they ask. The lawyers in my family taught me that a good prosecutor never asks a question for which she could not supply the answer. We need to be able to speak clearly about how the gospel and wider biblical witness offers answers to the topics we dare to raise. How would you answer for yourself the tough questions posed earlier?

Speak the jury's language. In asking questions or offering answers, effective prosecutors are also very careful not to use too much legal or technical jargon. Similarly, our aim in conversation with people can't be to show how much we know about the Bible or theology. If our purpose is to renew the mind of the jury, we have to use the jury's language. Notice how Jesus consistently did this. When challenging fishermen to pursue a higher calling, he invited them to become "fishers of people." When trying to reach a thirsty Samaritan woman, he spoke of "living water." When prosecuting his case with rural people, Jesus spoke of the kingdom of God in terms of sheep and seeds. We see the same sensitivity in the apostle Paul. When addressing Jews, Paul made his case by invoking the history of Israel. When speaking with a Gentile audience in Athens, he quoted Greek philosophers (Acts 17). If Jesus or Paul were talking to Gary today, who knows, they might even speak in terms of dentistry. What is certain is that they would speak in terms he would understand.

> HOW, THEN, CAN THEY CALL ON THE ONE THEY HAVE NOT BELIEVED IN? AND HOW CAN THEY BELIEVE IN THE ONE OF WHOM THEY HAVE NOT HEARD? AND HOW CAN THEY HEAR WITHOUT SOMEONE PREACHING TO THEM?
>
> Romans 10:14

DEFENSE TESTIMONY

The apostle Jude once wrote to the church: "Dear friends, I had been eagerly planning to write to you about the salvation we all share. But now I find that I must write about something else, urging you to *defend* the faith that God has entrusted once for all time to his holy people" (Jude 3 NLT, italics mine). Jude says he would far prefer to spend his energies communicating the good news of the salvation God has made possible through Jesus Christ. He was aware, however, of how many people's minds were being captured by a tide of teaching that was keeping them from pursuing the way of Christ. It left him with the feeling that what was urgently needed were Christian disciples who could "defend the faith."

Recognize the urgency. I can resonate with Jude. I would much rather devote my conversations with nondisciples to the saving power I've seen in the gospel. But I meet so many who are like the small tree beneath the shadow of the towering pine described in the last chapter. Their growth is blocked by large intellectual obstacles. They wonder, *How can there be a loving God in a world of such suffering? How can the Bible be true if Darwin was right? How could Christianity be good, given all the terrible things done in its name?* Some people will not progress until their minds get better light on these issues.

Aspire to be an apologist. This is why "defending testimony" is a very important part of Christian witness. Historically, the term for this kind of witness has been "apologetics," from the Greek word *apologia*, meaning "defense." When we hear this word today we often think of our contemporary term "apology," as in, "I'm sorry. I was wrong." In the classical sense, however, when people offered an *apologia*, it meant just the opposite. It was a way of saying, "I'm sorry, but I believe you may have heard wrong." Apologetics is the art of presenting a reasoned defense of one's belief with the intention of persuading the other person to join your side.

> THE MULTITUDES CANNOT KNOW THE GOSPEL UNLESS THEY HAVE A LIVING WITNESS. MERELY GIVING THEM AN EXPLANATION WILL NOT SUFFICE. THE WANDERING MASSES MUST HAVE A DEMONSTRATION OF WHAT TO BELIEVE—THEY MUST HAVE A MENTOR WHO WILL STAND AMONG THEM AND SAY, "FOLLOW ME, I KNOW THE WAY."
>
> Robert E. Coleman

Educate yourself. Some of us need to become better apologists for the faith. To do this, we need to invest more time getting answers for ourselves about some of the questions skeptics ask, questions which we may in fact have as well. When I walked into my freshman dorm room at Yale, I had been a Christian for all of three weeks. My roommates included a disaffected Catholic, an atheist and a Jewish man. We came to love one another, but they first attacked my faith like wolves on fresh meat. Some of my professors made my roommates look like toothless Chihuahuas.

I realized I would have to "eat or be eaten." I chose the former. I began to read voraciously and to consume the counsel of the smartest Christian mentors I could find. I now know that there are not only reasonable defenses to be given to the issues nondisciples raise, there is a staggering weight of science, history, philosophy, social science and more that aligns with God's revealed truth in Scripture. Do you know this for yourself? At the end of this book, you'll find a list of additional resources that will be well worth your investment. Pick up a few of them. Read them. Get clear on their content. Talk the material through with other disciples. Pass them on to others.

Be discerning about people. When talking with people, Michael Simpson, a respected author on the subject of evangelism, encourages us to distinguish between "firm" and "flexible" nondisciples.[2] The *firm* nondisciple is someone who holds an articulate and well-defined belief system. If you can engage them in a well-reasoned and informed argument, or hand them resources that will challenge and stretch their thinking, it is well worth your time. While this is not the only way to change the mind of a disciple, I know many earnest truth-seekers for whom this kind of discussion and resourcing eventually won the case.

Flexible nondisciples, on the other hand, are people whose disbelief has less to do with a particular worldview that is open to debate than with a personal lifestyle or set of feelings about Christianity or religion that create a visceral resistance to faith. Perhaps they don't want to stop sleeping around or partying hard. Maybe they've been hurt or judged by Christians. They may have experienced believers as shallow, hypocritical or unconcerned with the serious problems of the world. Trying to convince a flexible nondisciple of the existence of God or the authority of Scripture may actually be counterproductive. While these intellectual issues may be their presenting objection to faith, they are not the core of their disbelief. Arguing intellectual issues may actually set the relationship back because such persons may not be all that informed on these subjects and end up feeling more defensive or disrespected the further you press into them. To build a redemptive relationship with this kind of person involves understanding better what it was about the form of Christianity they met which turned their heart away. What set them to reaching for intellectual arguments to justify what is really a gut-level distaste?

Keep returning to Jesus. I have found that while many nondisciples I've talked with can come up with a list of reasons for rejecting Christianity or theism in general, few of them are repulsed by Jesus. I may meet resistance when discussing intellectual or lifestyle matters, but when I turn to talking about the person of Jesus, the tension dissipates, and they begin to display a greater openness.

Philip Yancey recounts the story of George Buttrick, for many years the chaplain at Harvard and a great defender of the faith. Whenever a student said: "I don't believe in God," Buttrick's standard reply was: "Why don't you sit down and tell me *what kind of God* you don't believe in. I probably don't believe in that God either." Buttrick would then go on to talk to the student about Jesus—the true corrective to all false notions of God. Yancey confesses: "I must admit that Jesus has revised in flesh many of my harsh and unpalatable notions about God . . . [Jesus is] brilliant, untamed, tender, creative, slippery, irreducible, paradoxically humble—Jesus stands up to scrutiny. He is who I want my God to be."[3]

PERSONAL TESTIMONY

Somehow, you came to a confession like Yancey's. To quote St. Paul, "God, who said, 'Let light shine out of darkness,' made his light shine in [your] heart to give [you] the light of the knowledge of the glory of God in the face of Christ" (2 Corinthians 4:6). This, above all else, is the reality to which you are called to testify. *Prosecuto-*

rial testimony is important; but there will always be those who have an airtight defense against the kind of spiritual case offered by even the most scintillating speaker or polished evangelist. *Defensive* testimony is needed too; but there will always be some who will be able to come up with objections to intellectual arguments for the Christian faith.

Hear this clearly. The majority of people in our time are not so much asking for a *description* of what the gospel is as they are seeking a compelling picture of the *difference* it makes. This is where *personal* testimony comes in. You will probably never have as great an opportunity to reshape the thoughts and feelings of a nondisciple with whom you've been walking and investigating as when that person actually *invites you* to take the stand.

Provide glowing doorknobs. Jesus once said, "I stand at the door and knock. If anyone hears my voice and opens the door, I will come in and eat with him, and he with me" (Revelation 3:20). Elsewhere he said, "Seek and you will find" (Matthew 7:7). Sometimes people just need help developing the curiosity to actually open the door to the kind of testimony through which Jesus makes his presence felt. We can catalyze that curiosity by providing what I call "glowing doorknobs." Let me illustrate.

My friend George travels a lot on business and meets all kinds of people. When they ask, "What do you do?" he often replies, "I'm a secret agent." People usually laugh and then say, "No, really, what's your job?" He follows up by saying, "Well, actually, my cover is working as a furniture salesman, but my real job is trying to help people fulfill their spiritual potential." At this point, the conversation hits a crucial pause. The word "spiritual" is a "glowing doorknob." It is a conversational invitation to engage in a discussion of spiritual matters, presented in such a way as to be nonconfrontational. The one invited to grasp the doorknob and walk through the door is free to walk away, and free to continue to converse. Other similarly charged words include *God, Jesus, Holy Spirit, Bible, ministry, church, conversion, life-changing, prayer, religion* and *faith*.

Some people see a glowing doorknob

> EVANGELISM CONVERSATION IS MUCH LIKE INVITING SOMEONE DOWN A LONG HALLWAY WITH DOORS LINING BOTH SIDES. IN MOST CASES, YOU HAVE NO WAY OF KNOWING WHERE THE SEEKER WILL STOP, INDICATING A DOORWAY INTO HIS OR HER HEART. THAT'S WHY OPENING MANY DOORS OF POTENTIAL CONVERSATION IS CRITICAL TO DISCOVERING SOMEONE'S DESIRES. NOT ALL SEEKERS ARE ATTRACTED TO THE SAME DOORS.
>
> Michael Simpson

and perceive danger there: "There's *fire* on the other side of that door!" They back away from conversation with George and he lets them, the same way Jesus did with those who heard his parables and chose not to ask more. People who are ready for spiritual conversation, however, tend to grab hold of the doorknob and turn it. They may respond to George, saying, "That's interesting. Tell me more." This opens up a whole new world of conversation.

Let me offer a few more examples of how this kind of glowing doorknob opportunity might work.

Barbara goes on short-term mission trips once or twice every year. When workmates ask her where she's going, she responds, "I'm taking a vacation with a purpose." The word "purpose" is another glowing doorknob, but one that few people think too hot to handle. "What purpose?" they'll ask. Barbara says something like, "Well, I'm involved with a community of people trying to make a difference in the world." "What kind of community or what kind of difference?" people inquire. "It's a group of people trying to live more like Jesus. Jesus has a heart for kids and the poor, so we try to change the lives of poor kids." Again, there's a pause. People either grab the doorknob or choose to pass it by. Many times, Barbara finds the door opening up.

At a cocktail party, Frank hears someone bemoaning the poor behavior of someone else. "Do you believe that guy did that?" Frank responds, "I actually do. I was a lot like that guy for a lot of years. I'd

probably still be that way if I hadn't had an experience that changed me significantly." Some people will be curious and ask what the experience was or how it changed him. Frank then talks a bit about his faith-awakening or one of the ways he feels God has altered him.

Do you get the picture? Offering statements that contain a glowing doorknob gives seekers access to a larger room with the opportunity to explore faith in Christ. Whether they turn that handle or not is their business and God's.

Talk less, listen more. Some time ago, I was called to testify in a serious legal proceeding. In preparing me, my lawyer said: "Keep your answers short. Don't offer more than you are asked. Make them ask follow-up questions." This is very helpful advice on the personal witness stand too. How many of us have lost someone's attention because we gave them "too much information"? We have to be willing to go slowly and let the other person's interest determine the rate and depth of the conversation. You want people to know that they have control of how much they hear. When they feel that you have enough "gentleness and respect" (1 Peter 3:15) not to tell them more than they've asked for, they may be much more likely to ask for more.

Don't force it. Perhaps you've seen TV courtroom dramas where a witness didn't say everything he or she wanted to and seemed to "clutch" after the receding attorney. As in the TV show, this behavior is often unhelpful, and may seem desperate, possibly damaging one's credibility. Consider the example of the rich young ruler—though Jesus loved him, he let the man go (Mark 10:17-22). Even though the Pharisees desperately needed the transformation Christ offered, Jesus did not press them beyond their willingness to hear. Jesus told his disciples to shake the dust from their feet and move on wherever they encountered people who didn't welcome their witness (Matthew 10:14). Don't sin against the Holy Spirit or harden the ground by pridefully pressing in where God has not readied the soil of someone's soul.

Stick to what you know. If you get on a witness stand in a court of law, you will be expected to "tell the truth, the whole truth, and nothing but the truth," or at least what measure of it you personally know. If you start to talk about anything other than what you have personally seen, heard, touched, felt or done, the opposing counsel is likely to say: "Objection, your honor, that's hearsay." The jury may then be instructed to ignore the testimony.

This is liberating, isn't it? It means that if you are in conversation with a non-disciple who makes an assertion or asks you a question about an area in which you feel you don't have the enough information, you are free to say, "I don't know." You will likely want to do some research once you get off the stand so that you have a meaningful answer the next time that topic comes up. But this is much better than blathering on about subjects where your relative ignorance or appearance of insincerity or insecurity damages the credibility of your witness.

Conversely, remember that great power lies in testifying to what you *do* know. It is very hard to argue with somebody who can authentically say, "I was blind but now I see" (John 9:25). Almost anyone will say in response to a confession like this, "Please tell me more."

WHEN YOU HAVE THE JURY'S ATTENTION . . .

If you have been faithful in pursuing the path of witness described in this book thus far, there is going to come a moment when you will have the jury's attention. Somebody you have been building a redemptive relationship with is going to ask: "What's your story? How did you get this faith, this knowledge, this life you seem to have?" What they may not say out loud, but may well have on their mind is, "How could it happen for me?"

Your job in that moment is not to answer the second question, but to respond to the first in a way that will indirectly begin to picture for the other the answer to the deeper question. Your ability to do this well with people will get stronger over time if you will follow a pattern of *preparing, sharing and repairing.* Let's consider each of those practices in turn.

1. Prepare your testimony. The apostle Peter wrote: "Always be prepared to give an answer to everyone who asks you to give the reason for the hope that you have" (1 Peter 3:15). Any other good lawyer would say the same: Prepare your testimony in advance so that you can offer it in a clear and winsome way when the door opens up. In the application exercise at the end of this chapter, you'll be encouraged to do this. To prime that process, think about three key phases of your journey.

- *Summarize your past.* Consider these questions: Before you became a disciple of Christ, what experiences shaped your understanding of God and life? Who were your positive or negative role models? If you went to church, what was that like? Did God seem absent, distant, an occasional presence or close to you? What did you hunger or hope for during this part of your journey? Where were you caught up in damaging patterns or poor priorities? In what did you put your faith, your source of identity or hope for fulfillment along the way? If you have walked with Christ since childhood, where have you struggled with doubts, failure, guilt or vain pursuits?

- *Describe your conversion.* Was there one decisive moment or a series of moments when God truly reached you? When did God wake you up to the need for a significant change in your understanding of him, yourself or the life he wanted for you? What circumstances or people did God use to bring you to faith in him? What were the questions or truths that God impressed on you at those times? How did you come to see a providential pattern of grace reaching out to you? Who helped you take the most important steps?

- *Identify the fruit.* How is your life differ-

ent today because of the impact of the gospel on you? What difference does being right with God make in your sense of peace and hope? How have you seen the Holy Spirit helping you to overcome specific character flaws? What are one or two areas in which God's truth has reset your course in life? Where do you see yourself now participating in God's redemptive effort to bring about change in this world? How has knowing you will have life beyond the grave altered your experience of suffering and loss in this life? How have you felt God's love filling you or reshaping the nature of your relationships with others? What has being part of a community of faith meant to you?

2. Share your testimony. When someone turns the doorknob and pulls the door wide open, asking to know your personal story, here's what you do.

- *Ask the Advocate for help.* Jesus promised that "when the Advocate comes . . . the Spirit of truth who comes from the Father, he will testify on my behalf" (John 15:26 NRSV). The Holy Spirit is most capable of planting truth in the soul of an individual (John 16:8). Ask the Spirit to guide your words and work his Word into the life of the person listening.

- *Don't worry about drama.* You don't have to have a spectacular "gutter-to-glory" story. The tale of someone who opened their heart to God at an early age and has been led along a winding trail of discovery, growth and service is a beautiful testimony too.

- *Keep your story brief.* The questions suggested above are to help you outline your story, not define all the details you should try to pack into your testimony. As Albert Einstein once said, "Things should be as simple as possible, but not simpler." Tell only as much as required to make clear the needs you have had, how God has met you there, and how he's been changing your character and life trajectory. Let the other person ask questions if they want to know more.

- *Key in on conversion influences.* If you are able to describe the crucial role that someone played in your faith development, it might occur to your listener that perhaps you are someone God has sent to play this kind of role in his or her life. You want them to see that there has been a providential pattern of grace reaching out to them too. Seeing the steps you took to respond to God's grace can create a picture of a pathway they might walk too.

- *Major on the A.D. not the B.C.* A lot of people tend to put too much emphasis on the Before Christ (B.C.) story, but not enough on the "After Discipleship" (A.D.) story. Be sure to spend as much or more time on the ongoing effects of God and his gospel in your life. As we'll see in the next chapter, this will be one of the most attractive elements of your witness.

- *Focus on feelings more than facts.* There are many fascinating details to the story of your life and God's work in it. As you tell this story, however, make sure the details don't overwhelm the dramatic core of what has happened in you. If you dwell a lot on *facts*—for example, the town you grew up in, the school you attended, the places you went—you may or may not touch similar aspects of your listener's life. If you focus instead on the *feelings* you had—your longings, fears, emptiness, pain, joys—you will almost certainly establish many powerful touch-points. What have you felt about your need and about God's grace?

- *Read your listener.* If you see someone nodding pensively, or even tearing up in response to what you are sharing, ask: "What have I said to cause you to feel this way?" The goal really isn't to finish telling *your* story; it is to get to the *other* person's story, to that place where God can meet their deepest needs. The converse is also possible. If you see the other person fidgeting or their eyes glazing over, pull back. Ask, "What's kicking up in you as I'm talking?" If necessary, don't hesitate to say, "There's more to the story for another day." They'll ask for more if or when they are ready.

3. Refine your testimony. Like every other important activity of your life, you will get better at telling your story through practice and coaching. Sit with another disciple or a group of them and share your stories with one another. Ask them, "What elements particularly connected with you and why? Where did I lose you? What do you wish I might have said differently, less or more?"

A FINAL THOUGHT

The greatest witnesses have always remembered that it is not so much the elo-quence of their prosecution, or the wisdom of their defense, as the trembling telling of a personal story about the God of redeeming love and power that has won the jury's faith (1 Corinthians 2:1-5). Go into the courtroom of this world, testifying to that story. God will use you to help some blind people see.

---

[1]Dallas Willard, *Renovation of the Heart: Putting on the Character of Christ* (Colorado Springs: NavPress, 2002).

[2]Michael L. Simpson, *Permission Evangelism: When to Talk, When to Walk* (Colorado Springs: Cook Communications, 2003), p. 30.

[3]Philip Yancey, *The Jesus I Never Knew* (Grand Rapids: Zondervan, 1995), p. 264.

Application Exercise

1. In the column to the left below, write down two tough questions (perhaps suggested by the Prosecutorial Testimony section of the reading) that you'd like to ask more often of nondisciples. In the column to the right, jot down a few notes to suggest something of what you might want to communicate to someone if a dialogue arose between you on these subjects.

Question	Christian Truth

2. List below two or three intellectually oriented questions you know that nondisciples may well ask you for which you'd like to get better prepared to give a Defense Testimony.

3. Jot down below a statement that might serve as a "curiosity catalyst" in some of your conversations with nondisciples. Circle the "glowing doorknob" words/phrases.

4. Write down below (or on a separate page) a very brief outline of your spiritual journey. Share it verbally with someone. Over the next few months, write out a longer response to the "Prepare Your Testimony" section of the reading.

5. List below several specific fruits of your relationship with Christ.

6. Does the reading convict, challenge or comfort you? Why?

Going Deeper

Little, Paul E. *How to Give Away Your Faith*. Downers Grove, IL: InterVarsity Press, 1988.

Simpson, Michael L. *Permission Evangelism: When to Talk, When to Walk*. Colorado Springs: Cook Communications, 2003.

See the additional resources list at the back of the book for more ideas.

8 / Nail the Sins That Slay You

LOOKING AHEAD

MEMORY VERSE: Luke 6:42
BIBLE STUDY: Colossians 3:1-17
READING: Beyond the Bumper

 Core Truth

What do we need to do with the character flaws that potentially compromise our witness?

Strengthening our credibility with others requires an honest awareness and open confession of our own untransformed character and a purposeful commitment to seeking the help of God and others in repairing these sins. As people see us clearly naming and sincerely crucifying the sins that limit our lives, they will become more interested in pursuing this pathway to authentic life-change for themselves.

1. Identify key words or phrases in the question and answer above, and state their meaning in your own words.

2. Restate the core truth in your own words.

3. What questions or issues does the core truth raise for you?

Memory Verse Study Guide

Copy the entire text here:

———————————————

———————————————

———————————————

———————————————

———————————————

———————————————

———————————————

———————————————

———————————————

———————————————

———————————————

———————————————

———————————————

———————————————

———————————————

———————————————

———————————————

———————————————

———————————————

Memory Verse: Luke 6:42

The credibility of our testimony is severely compromised if there is not integrity between our words and our deeds. Jesus says that before we presume to guide others, we need to look hard at our own inner life and make sure it is rooted in God in such a way that it bears the kind of fruit others would want for themselves.

1. *Putting it in context:* In Luke 6, Jesus offers a series of short teachings aimed at this theme of integrity. Read Luke 6:37-49. Put in your own words the one "big idea" that Jesus is advancing in these three short passages.

2. Based on what this passage says about judgment and grace, how would you describe the attitude that disciples are meant to bring to their interactions with other people (vv. 37-38)?

3. Why is it a problem when someone presumes to address the shortcomings of others without addressing their own first (vv. 39-42)?

4. According to Jesus, what determines the quality or character of a person's outside life (vv. 43-45)?

5. If we are truly being trained by Christ and not just taking his name in vain, what would one reasonably expect the outcome to be (v. 40)?

6. What does Jesus say is necessary for our lives to have the kind of structural integrity needed to stand up to the tests brought upon us by the scrutiny of others and life's storms (vv. 46-49)?

Inductive Bible Study Guide

Bible Study: Colossians 3:1-17

Sometimes Christians speak and behave as if Jesus has done all the dying necessary for us. While it is true that Jesus made the supreme sacrifice on the cross required for us to get right with God (justification), he clearly expects his followers to crucify sin in their lives (sanctification). The apostle Paul describes this ongoing process in Colossians 3.

1. *Read Colossians 3:1-4.* As disciples, we often hope for or expect a better character than we had before meeting Christ, or a better life in comparison to our life before we knew Christ. What does Paul say in these verses that our focus ought to be and why?

2. *Read Colossians 3:5.* What challenge is issued in this verse?

   What difficulties present themselves as you consider meeting the challenge?

3. *Read Colossians 3:5-11.* List the specific attributes of the "earthly nature" that we are called to "put to death" or rid ourselves of—in short, to nail to the cross?

   Which of these struggles seems the most difficult for you to overcome?

   How might you begin to address the issue or issues with which you struggle most?

4. *Read Colossians 3:12.* Paul says that Christ's followers are "holy" (that is, set apart for a significant purpose) and "dearly loved" (precious to God). How might this reality motivate you to want to overcome the sin in your life?

5. *Read Colossians 3:12-17.* List the specific attributes of character that will increasingly mark your life as you grow in Christ.

Which of these do you feel you most lack, and which do you most desire to have?

What steps can you take to begin developing these qualities?

6. If these qualities were abundant in your life, how might that affect other people's openness to what you had to say about God and life?

7. What questions or issues does this passage raise for you?

Reading: Beyond the Bumper

MISTAKEN IDENTITY

At a crowded traffic intersection, a stoplight turns from red to green. The young man driving the first car in line is busy texting and fails to notice the change. This prompts the driver in the second car to begin pounding on his steering wheel in frustration. When the first driver still doesn't move, the man behind erupts in rage. As the light turns yellow, the man leans on his car horn and starts shouting obscenities out the window. Jolted by the commotion, the first driver looks up, sees the yellow light and accelerates through the intersection *just* as the light turns red.

> THE MARK OF A SAINT IS NOT PERFECTION BUT CONSECRATION. A SAINT IS NOT A MAN WITHOUT FAULTS, BUT A MAN WHOSE HEART HAS BEEN GIVEN WITHOUT RESERVE TO GOD.
>
> Brooke Foss Westcott

The second driver is practically bursting a blood vessel now. In the midst of his ranting, he looks out his window and into the face of a very serious-looking policeman. The officer promptly arrests him, handcuffs him and takes him to the police station for booking.

An hour or two later, the driver is led back to the booking desk where the original officer is waiting. "I'm really sorry for this mistake," the officer says. "You see, I pulled up behind your car while you were blowing your horn, flipping that driver off and cussing a blue streak. Then I noticed the 'What Would Jesus Do?' bumper sticker. I saw the fish emblem on the trunk. I just assumed that you had stolen the car."

UNTRANSFORMED CHRISTIANS

Like the policeman in this story, most nondisciples think it reasonable to expect those who bear the name of Jesus to behave something like their Master, even amidst the frustrations of this life. What makes belief difficult, however, is the experience they have with *untransformed Christians*. They've met too many Christians who act as if righteousness were mainly about ranting and raving over the sin in other people's lives instead of nailing and negating it in their own.

This phenomenon clearly concerned Jesus too. Jesus does not ask us to do more than he himself did; but he did say that while "a student is not *above* his teacher . . . everyone who is fully trained will be *like* his teacher" (Luke 6:40, italics mine). In other words, if you are setting your course by Christ's truth, then you won't need bumper stickers (or anything else) to prove how godly you are. You will increasingly move through life like Jesus is at the wheel.

To drive this point home, Jesus employs another agricultural metaphor: "No good tree bears bad fruit, nor does a bad tree bear good fruit. Each tree is recognized by its own fruit. People do not pick figs from thornbushes, or grapes from briers" (Luke 6:43-44). Jesus is saying that people won't come to you for compassion or love if they believe you to be a prickly, cruel or unwelcoming person. They will want what you offer only if they view you as someone whose heart is filled with good (Luke 6:45). For this reason, the Bible exhorts us, "Above all else, guard your heart, for it is the wellspring of life" (Proverbs 4:23). Let's think about what is required to do this.

AT WORK BENEATH THE SURFACE

Some time ago, I traded in my beat-up old car for a model with a body so beautiful and an engine so pristine that I could hardly believe it had only 50,000 miles on it. Within a week, however, the car began stuttering and an amber service light appeared on the dash. Because the car's dealer is legendary for service, I took the vehicle back immediately. The mechanic opened the hood in front of me. He then proceeded to unfasten and remove what I *only then* realized was simply the dust cover for the actual heart of the car. Underneath the cover, the engine block looked all of its mileage. I flushed in humiliation, realizing that I'd bought the car without ever seeing the actual engine. After a good look, however, the mechanic had nailed the problem. "Look here," he said. "A hose is coming loose. We'll get to work on that."

Check your engine. There is a helpful analogy here. If our witness is to be effective, then we need to pay much less attention to the bumpers, upholstery and dust covers of our lives than to the condition of our engine. Thankfully, Jesus tells us exactly how our heart is supposed to work if everything is running according to the Creator's original specifications.

Jesus said that when everything is running right we will operate as servants and stewards instead of as masters and consumers (Matthew 21:33-41). We'll be far more concerned with asking how we can be a good neighbor to others than with judging their neighborliness (Luke 10:25-37). Jesus said that if our heart is good, we'll be willing to take up a cross to bring forth the best, rather than run from sacrifice (Mark 8:31-37). We'll be oriented more toward investing the gifts we've been given for the purposes of God than with hoarding them (Luke 12:16-31; Matthew 25:14-30). Jesus told us that we will forgive others generously, rather than keeping tallies, simply because we know how great a debt God has forgiven us (Matthew 18:23-35). He said that rather than having our engines racing with anxiety and fear, we will face difficulties and even death itself with a sense of peace, knowing that we're in the hands of a very loving God (Matthew 6:25-30).

Is this the way your heart is operating? The truth for most of us is that the miles take a deadly toll on our engines. The sludge of pride or rage builds up within us.

Deceit, gluttony or sloth clog our system. Lust and envy have a way of corroding our heart connections. We take in a lot of tainted fuel in this world; the seasons of life can be harsh on a heart.

Note warning signs. Maybe you've been ignoring a warning light on the dashboard of a key relationship or your own physical health. Something or someone has been trying to tell you that a fix is needed, but you've been telling yourself, "It can't be happening," or "Not so soon," or "I'll get to it one of these days." Perhaps you've been driving the way you have for so long and in a lane next to so many people whose engines are performing the same way as yours is that you think, "This must be how life is supposed to work." It takes humility to face the reality that your engine's knocking or stuttering. It requires courage to nail the sin that hurts our character and slays our witness with others.

Admit your need. One of my critics once said, "Dan, there are some things about you that are never going to change because you just can't see them." When I asked why he thought that was, he said, "Because you are using those things to see." I sat for a long time with that idea. Is it possible that there are problems with my character so large and dominating that they have blocked my ability to accurately evaluate myself? In time, I realized that the answer was yes. A whole host of sins were corrupting my vision of myself and limiting my ability to be of help to others as they work through their areas of weakness (Matthew 7:4-5).

This is why Jesus asks: "Can a blind man lead a blind man? Will they not both fall into a pit?" (Luke 6:39). He knows that some of us have huge hunks of rotting wood in our self-awareness or way of living. Some nondisciples look at us and think, "If that's the Christian life, I don't want it." Admitting this reality is hard, but it is the essential first step to a better character and witness.

Get to the mechanic. The second step is to bring the engine into the shop for repair. This is one of the major reasons why the wisest disciples have always put a high priority on gathering regularly to worship God and grow in the community of other believers. They go to have their hearts and minds recalibrated by God's truth. They go to be cleaned by confession and lubed by God's forgiveness. They seek out the community of faith because they realize that they need others to help them see where they may have gotten sludged up. Are *you* in worship regularly? Do you have a small group of other disciples to whom you regularly open yourself?

Keep the supply lines attached. When I brought my car in for repair, the mechanic pointed out that I had a hose coming loose. At the time I thought of it as a minor problem. In reality, however, this little issue was a very big problem. The hoses in a car supply gas that keeps the carburetor firing, oil

> ONLY THOSE WHO ARE LOST
>
> WILL FIND THE PROMISED LAND.
>
> Abraham Heschel

that keeps the engine running, fluid that keeps the brakes working and liquid that keeps the windshield clean. These little hoses are huge assets in the proper operation of an automobile.

Our Creator made each of us in such a way that his power only flows fully through us when certain "spiritual hoses" are well connected. As we touched on in chapter two, Christians have historically called these the *spiritual disciplines*. It is through the conduits of these disciplines that God moves the living water of his Spirit into all the parts of the "car" of our character. Perhaps you've been driving so fast for so long over life's rugged roads that some of these key spiritual hoses have gotten dislodged. Maybe they never got connected properly in the first place.

Most twenty-first-century people are aware of very few spiritual disciplines, much less practicing them. Lacking the means to maintain a vital daily connection with Christ, many disciples therefore make little progress in character development. At the end of this chapter, I've suggested several manuals to help you install a few more hoses than may be in place right now. Do this, and over time you'll start to see your heart, mind, soul and strength operating in a way you might never have thought possible (Mark 12:30-31). More importantly, you will develop a character that will make those who watch you want to turn to Christ as well.

MY STORY: BEFORE CHRIST

As easily as I describe this vision now, it has taken me a long time to understand all this for myself. It has taken longer still to grasp that it is okay for me and other would-be witnesses to humbly and honestly show the people who watch our journey through life that we know it is still far from perfect. It is not just okay for us to do that. It is essential. Permit me to lead us further into that dimension of witness by sharing with you more of my own story.

Family: Great expectations. I grew up the eldest son of an elder brother in a family of very "accomplished" people. There were at least three generations of my elders at Princeton and Yale. As far as I could tell, almost all of them became a Wall Street tycoon, real estate baron, corporate executive or government leader. A dominant feeling of my childhood was fear that I would be the one to break this family pattern. I wasn't a gifted athlete or a particularly good-looking boy. I was a good student, but it upset me that a B or even an A-minus on a report card became the focus of concern in my family, a sign of failure. I came to dread the question, "What happened in *that* class?"

Values: Winning the game. One was not allowed to hold on to hurt or anger in my family—at least not openly. I recall wrestling with my father when I was small, getting knocked down and starting to cry. Dad said, "Hold on. If you cry, you lose the game." I don't blame him for this now. It was a lesson he'd been taught by his own parents and was just passing along to me. I learned that being athletic or attractive makes you popular. I absorbed the message that you shouldn't feel too good about any report card that isn't perfect. I came to believe that if you want to be a winner you are not to show any weakness or vulnerability.

God: Demanding perfection. We went to a couple of churches when I was young, but I got the impression that the rules there were about the same as my family's rules. God also had very high expectations. Church people seemed to care a lot about climbing ladders and looking good. They gave out chocolate for memorizing Bible verses—a place to win. By the time I finished middle school, however, church was no longer a weekly experience. Dad had been elected to the state legislature and weekends got busier. I got good at dressing up and impressing voters. I learned how important it is to appear very good in public.

Aspiration: Becoming Atlas. As I entered high school, I became a disciple of Ayn Rand, an articulate atheist whose books became my new Bible. Rand's characters are like the Greek hero Atlas— granite-jawed titans, able to carry immense weight without sweating. They don't cry or need other people. They are loners who simply create, build and achieve. I wanted to be like this, but was not. I felt lonely, anxious and weak. I'd begun cheating now and then to improve my scores. I exaggerated my accomplishments frequently. I had started stealing from my parents' alcohol closet. I was becoming a very "complicated" teenager.

Success: Serving the gods. Even when you are an atheist, as I was by then, you have "gods" that you serve. Everyone has *an* "ultimate authority" that they trust and obey in the hope of finding security, identity and fulfillment (1 Peter 3:15). My gods at this point were material goods, family image and popularity. As I entered my senior year, they were at the height of their glory. I was living in a nine-bedroom home on a ten-acre estate. I was part of a picture-perfect family and Dad was running for Congress. I was an A-student and a varsity basketball player, and was dating the captain of the cheerleading squad. I felt like I might just fulfill all those great expectations after all.

> WE ARE NOT RESPONSIBLE FOR OUTSIDERS' DECISIONS, BUT WE ARE ACCOUNTABLE WHEN OUR ACTIONS AND ATTITUDES— MISREPRESENTING A HOLY, JUST, AND LOVING GOD—HAVE PUSHED OUTSIDERS AWAY. OFTEN CHRISTIANITY'S NEGATIVE IMAGE REFLECTS REAL PROBLEMS, ISSUES THAT CHRISTIAN NEED TO OWN AND BE ACCOUNTABLE TO CHANGE.
>
> David Kinnaman

MY STORY: CONVERSION

In one of his most famous parables, Jesus said that every one of us has three things in common: (1) all of us spend our lives building a *house*—a structure that embodies our hope for the satisfaction of our longings; (2) everyone chooses a *foundation* for this house we are building—a platform made up of whatever we believe will secure the fulfillment of that hope; (3) everyone faces *storms* that reveal the strength of the foundation we chose (Matthew 7:24-29).

Storms come. During my senior year in high school, the storms came. My father lost his race for Congress. My parents separated the next day and would be divorced several months later. Our house went up in a terrible fire. And I finally came to terms with a fact I did not want to face: my maternal grandfather—an icon of the life I was hoping to build for myself—had somehow, beneath the surface of a life that *looked* very good, actually been so miserable that he chose to end his life. My heart's engine died. The house came crashing down. The gods of material goods, family image and popularity proved to be little more than sand.

I felt bitterly angry and confused about what or who to trust. I shut down, refused to talk to most of my friends and was unwilling to let them see me cry. Instead, I stepped up my abuse of drugs and alcohol in an effort to anaesthetize myself. I was utterly godless and lost.

Seeker of the lost. What I had no capacity to understand at that moment is that there exists in this universe Someone with a rather remarkable heart for lost coins, lost sheep and especially lost

kids. Fortunately, he had already found my father again. In a remarkable act of parental force, my dad came to me that summer and told me that he was sending me to a Christian camp in North Carolina. I protested violently. The last thing I wanted to do was waste my few days before college in the company of a bunch of pale hypocrites who believed in some fantasy God. But my father held the financial keys to the "kingdom of college" and he would not back down.

A different kind of Christian. I had never met Christians like the people at that camp. Maybe I had encountered them at other times and I simply didn't have the eyes to see them. I know now that what I was meeting in them was the fruit of the Spirit (Galatians 5:22-23). They knew how to laugh at themselves and make me laugh. I tried to push them away, but they didn't get ruffled by how difficult I was. They just kept engaging me in conversation, listening to my questions and criticisms of Christianity, and offering answers that increasingly made more sense. There was a deep joy and confidence in these people that I found very attractive.

A Jesus I would follow. They also talked about a Jesus I had never known. He was not the "Jesus meek and mild" I'd heard about in Sunday school as a child, but a man of stunning strength mixed with amazing compassion. He made powerful, selfish people anxious and ordinary, humble people comfortable. But Jesus also made outrageous claims about himself—to be able to forgive sins, overcome death and give people life beyond this world. I had so many doubts, but I became fascinated with this Jesus. He pictured the kind of world I wanted to live in and the kind of God I would want to have if one existed.

The power of the gospel. Toward the end of the week, the leaders at the camp talked about how Jesus died to take the punishment that human sin deserved and heal the breach between people and God. The description they gave of what he went through on the cross and the way he asked God to forgive the people doing this to him choked me up. They detailed the evidence for the resurrection and I was shocked at how compelling it seemed to be. One of the leaders I liked most described the changes that came over the character of the disciples as the Holy Spirit filled them—and the ways his life had changed since asking Christ to come and fill his heart. I didn't want to admit it to anyone, but I felt, *I so need changing.*

A skeptic's prayer. At the close of the camp, one of the speakers issued an invitation for us to ask Jesus into our hearts if we had never done so before. I didn't go forward as others did, but inside of me something happened. I could feel God there in that room. I could sense him looking at me. It felt like he was saying, "Now is the time, Dan. I've been looking after you and for you all of your life. Let me show what I can do with you." I answered silently, "God, if that is really you . . . If you really exist, then please hear this prayer. I

know my life is empty and messed up. If it is possible for me to have what these people seem to have, if it is possible to know you and be changed by you like these people say, then come into my heart and show me the next step."

My Story: After Discipleship Began

It has been many years since I said those things to God. Jesus has led me many steps since then. His Spirit guided me to a Christian fellowship in college and called me back to himself the many times I have strayed. Over the years, he's led me to several different churches—none perfect, but each crucial in my faith development. God has brought a variety of mentors and messengers into my life to teach me what I needed to know at just the right time. I have rarely gone a week without meeting with some small group of other disciples. The spiritual hoses I mentioned earlier have been indispensable in my growth too.

Storms still come. Knowing Christ has not stopped more painful storms from coming my way. But he has been the firm foundation that has allowed the new house of hope he's building in me to remain standing despite the maelstrom. Nothing has been wasted. Every experience, whether painful or happy—all the way back to when I was born and all the way forward to the time I die—has, I believe, been woven into his wise and gracious plan (Romans 8:28). As many people have said before, God is good all the time.

Still a sinner. But the closer to Jesus I

get, the more aware I feel of the size of the gap between how very good he is and how sinful I am. I'm still far too prone to a perfectionism that is more about earning approval than it is about becoming Christlike. There are too many times when my pride fills me with the grandiose notion that my opinion is more important than someone else's. I am ashamed of how deceitfully I tend to spin events to make me look better than I am, or make up excuses when I have genuinely dropped the ball. There is still a level of anxiety in me that tells me I haven't put enough trust in God.

Still learning. These are just *some* of the things God and others have been able to help me face. There are surely many problems I haven't yet the vision to see. But I know that God can still help me to change for his glory and for the benefit of others as well as myself. I remain so thankful for the patience that God and others continue to show with the pace of my sanctification process.

The work of the Savior. I feel profoundly grateful for the changes Christ has brought about in me over the years. He took a very lonely, hardened, selfish young man and has transformed his heart in many ways. God has grown in me a genuine love and compassion for people that was simply absent before. He has made me gentler toward my critics and desirous of reconciliation with my enemies. It is a gift from above. It didn't start with me.

Joy is a much deeper and more frequent experience than ever before. I have bad days like anyone else, but I wake up most mornings feeling genuinely hopeful. I believe God is going to be active throughout the day and will provide me with opportunities to cooperate with his good work, if I pay attention. I feel passionate about participating in God's redemptive movement in this world. Giving money or time to this work isn't for appearances or a tax deduction but because *his* generous spirit moves in me now. I want to give a gift that matters and sow a seed that continues. I view my family, workplace and community involvements as great places to do that.

As much as anxiety is still too active in me, there is also much greater peace. It is much less difficult for me to admit when I'm wrong, confess where I'm struggling or acknowledge where I need help. I don't care to be Atlas anymore. I just want to be a person who, by the end of life's journey, is a lot more like Jesus than when I first heard his call to discipleship in that mountain camp so many years ago.

TRANSFORMING CHRISTIANS

Can you imagine opening up your life to nondisciples in this sort of way? I've shared with you my story partly to illustrate what a full-bodied testimony might look like along the lines we have explored. But I also do it to make vivid what it looks like to "nail the sins that slay us." To nail sin means: (1) to name it clearly and (2) to crucify it sincerely (Colossians 3:5). This is something to which Christians in our time have not been sufficiently committed. We too easily settle into the role of moral traffic cop for others. We too easily entrust our witness to the bumper stickers. The way we drive isn't sufficiently different from that of the drivers around us.

The need today. What the world needs now are transforming Christians—people who are honest about the problems they have and who are committed to seeking help to fix them. It needs people who understand that while Jesus did the ultimate atoning work upon the cross, his sacrifice was intended to inspire a commitment among his followers to keep dying to sin themselves (Mark 8:34). Our world needs disciples who are clear that while "Jesus is the same yesterday and today and forever" (Hebrews 13:8), the program for the rest of us is difficult but glorious change (2 Corinthians 3:17-18).

Is change possible? Most everyone wonders, *Is it really possible for me to change? Is there a power that can help me overcome my character flaws?* Be part of the reason they come to believe that the answer is yes. As others share their vulnerabilities with you, look for opportunities to name with some of your nondisciple friends the sins with which you've regularly struggled. Talk about how God is helping you put those to death, or how you long for this to happen. Imagine yourself saying things like: "I'm so sorry that I responded like that in the meeting earlier today. I have this problem with pride that I know God wants to

change. We've made some progress, but it's obvious there's more work to do. Forgive me." Or "I'm not sure my marriage would have made it if it weren't for the influence of Jesus on me. He's helped me see how lazy and demanding I can be. I've asked him to help repair those flaws." Or "I haven't been the best parent at times. Knowing how God loves his children has really challenged me to try to love my kids more like that. I'm working at that now." As natural openings present themselves, actually nail the truth in this kind of way.

Our transforming hope. The sort of self-awareness and confession that we've explored here will not invalidate your witness with people; it will dramatically improve it. They will know you are a real person and not their judge. They will become curious about the path of authentic life change you appear to be on. Through it you will show people the Jesus who is still a friend to sinners and who wills to help even the worst of us become someone better (1 Timothy 1:15-16). One day some of those who watch your witness will open their lives to God's renewing Spirit. To paraphrase Dr. Martin Luther King Jr., they will join you in saying: "I know I am not the person I ought to be. I know I'm not the person I want to be. I know I'm not the person I'm going to be. But as I sit at this stoplight today, I thank God Almighty, I am not the person I once was."

Application Exercise

1. Where, if at all, did you resonate with any elements of the author's personal story?

2. Which of the following areas of sin do you sense still needs to be crucified more fully in you and where do you see it manifesting itself?

☐ Pride— ☐ Gluttony—

☐ Envy— ☐ Sloth—

☐ Lust— ☐ Deceit—

☐ Anger— ☐ Anxiety/Fear—

☐ Greed— ☐ Other—

3. How often do you take yourself "into the shop," where others can help you check and repair the car of your character?

(0 – Never; 1 = Rarely; 2 = Occasionally; 3 = Frequently; 4 = Consistently)

_____ I let God tune my heart, recalibrate my mind and renew my soul through experiences of worshiping him.

_____ I open myself to a small group of other disciples, welcoming them to help me identify places in need of repair.

4. Put a *check mark* next to the spiritual disciplines that you use to maintain your life-giving attachment to God when you are not in the "shop." *Circle* the ones about which you'd like to learn more. (The Going Deeper resources can help.)

_____	Bible Study	_____	Fasting	_____	Service
_____	Celebration	_____	Journaling	_____	Silence
_____	Confession	_____	Lectio Divina	_____	Simplicity
_____	Contemplation	_____	Prayer	_____	Slowing
_____	Detachment	_____	Rest	_____	Solitude
_____	Discernment	_____	Sabbath	_____	Submission
_____	Examen	_____	Secret Faithfulness	_____	Others . . .

5. List at least two aspects of your character that are different today because of Christ's renewing influence in your life.

6. Does the reading convict, challenge or comfort you? Why?

Going Deeper

Barton, Ruth Haley. *Sacred Rhythms: Arranging Our Lives for Spiritual Transformation.* Downers Grove, IL: InterVarsity Press, 2006.

Calhoun, Adele A. *Spiritual Disciplines Handbook: Practices That Transform Us.* Downers Grove, IL: InterVarsity Press, 2005.

Caliguire, Mindy. *Discovering Soul Care.* Downers Grove IL: InterVarsity Press, 2007.

Johnson, Jan. *Spiritual Disciplines Companion: Bible Studies and Practices to Transform Your Soul.* Downers Grove, IL: InterVarsity Press, 2009.

Smith, James Bryan. *The Good and Beautiful Life: Putting on the Character of Christ.* Downers Grove, IL: InterVarsity Press, 2009.

9 / Express Grace Under Pressure

LOOKING AHEAD

MEMORY VERSE: 2 Corinthians 1:12
BIBLE STUDY: 2 Corinthians 6:1-10
READING: When the Pressure Is On

 Core Truth

What life situations offer us significant opportunities to increase the appeal and influence of our Christian witness?

Our witness becomes dramatically more attractive and credible to nondisciples as they see us expressing unusual grace in the face of the crushing circumstances that often bring out the worst in people. If we can display a truly Christlike character when we are under pressure, it will create curiosity and conversation about our faith and values.

1. Identify key words or phrases in the question and answer above, and state their meaning in your own words.

2. Restate the core truth in your own words.

3. What questions or issues does the core truth raise for you?

Memory Verse Study Guide

Copy the entire text here:

_____

_____

_____

_____

_____

_____

_____

_____

_____

_____

_____

_____

_____

_____

_____

_____

_____

_____

_____

Memory Verse: 2 Corinthians 1:12

Throughout his second letter to the church at Corinth, the apostle Paul reminds us that to be a follower of Jesus means to live by a different set of motives and standards than is common in our world. This distinctiveness makes Christ's witnesses like "salt" and "light" that draw people's attention to God (Matthew 5:13-16).

1. *Putting it in context:* In 2 Corinthians 1, Paul describes the difference that the grace of God makes in the lives of his disciples. *Read 2 Corinthians 1:1-7.* When in your life have you especially needed God's compassion and comfort?

2. *Read 2 Corinthians 1:8.* How does Paul describe the conditions he and Timothy faced in the province of Asia and the early effect this experience had on them?

3. *Read 2 Corinthians 1:9-11*. What was the silver lining or opportunity contained in these experiences?

4. *Read 2 Corinthians 1:12*. What do Paul and Timothy "boast" in?

5. List below two or three life situations where living by "worldly wisdom" and living "according to God's grace" (v. 12) in the face of "great pressure" (v. 8) result in very different conduct?

Life Situation	By Worldly Wisdom	According to Grace

6. How would you describe the importance of being seen by nondisciples as someone who expresses God's grace when you are under pressure?

Inductive Bible Study Guide

Bible Study: 2 Corinthians 6:1-10

Being a follower of Jesus does not exempt us from facing the trials and troubles common to human life (John 16:33). By God's grace, however, Christ's disciples are enabled to live in such a way that even the pressures they endure become opportunities to commend the goodness of God and the beauty of the Christian life. In this passage, Paul pictures this reality vividly.

1. *Read 2 Corinthians 6:1-2.* What is Paul concerned that the Corinthians not receive "in vain" and what do you think he means by this (v. 1)?

2. *Read 2 Corinthians 6:3-4.* What seems to be Paul's passionate desire here with respect to how others view Christians?

3. Give an example of someone presenting a "stumbling block" to the development of other people's faith and of someone who "commends" the faith by the way they live?

4. *Read 2 Corinthians 6:4-10.* List a few of the heavy pressures Paul says were brought to bear on disciples in his time.

5. List some of the specific character traits Paul says those disciples expressed under this duress.

6. Of these various character attributes, which seem to you most likely to strike nondisciples as particularly commendable? Why might this be the case?

7. What questions or issues does this passage raise for you?

Reading: When the Pressure Is On

THE GRACE OF THE GREAT

In the last seconds of the first game of the 1997 NBA championship series, Michael Jordan snatched a pass from between the outstretched hands of two defenders. With the crowd in a frenzy, Jordan left the ground, rose to a seemingly impossible height and flipped his wrist. The ball spun from his fingers, arced across space and ripped through the net cords to win the game as the buzzer sounded. A few games later, with the championship series tied 2-2, Jordan came down with a devastating stomach flu. Michael not only went onto the court that night, he scored thirty-eight points, including the game-deciding three-pointer with only seconds left.

Now and then we catch a glimpse of other performances like this. We see it in the stage actress whose partner blows his line, bringing forth from her a magnificent improvisation better than the original script. We find it in the violinist who loses two strings in the middle of a concert yet, rather than quitting, finishes the piece by recomposing the music and playing brilliantly with what he has left. We view it in the artist who, having lost the use of her hands, learns to paint masterpieces with a brush poised in her teeth.

It is well known that the full fragrance of a flower or the true potential of a grape is not known until it is crushed. But it is like this with people too. This is the way with the "great ones": their real substance isn't seen until the moment of pressure. What comes out of them then is the very essence of grace.

THE GREATEST ONE

The life of Jesus was one long display of grace under pressure. He is our model as we consider what it means to maintain our witness most especially when we are under duress.

Grace in the midst of temptation. In the wilderness, Satan confronted Jesus with three of the most pressing temptations known to any of us. He called Christ to find his fulfillment in the feeding of his bodily appetites, to pursue power by any means possible and to stake his self-image in his capacity to work wonders that would wow the crowd. In each case, however, we see Jesus expressing faith in God, his Word and his way as the ultimate source of his fulfillment, influence, and identity (Luke 4:1-13).

Grace in the face of diversion. Again and again, Jesus is pressured by people to make

> IF OUR LIVES DO NOT GIVE TESTIMONY TO THE RADICAL DIFFERENCE THAT KNOWING CHRIST MAKES, OUR EVANGELISM WILL ULTIMATELY BE INEFFECTIVE AND HOLLOW.
>
> Becky Pippert

their agenda his. The clamoring crowd seeks to force him to become their political messiah (John 6:15). The people he feeds try to turn him into their permanent social welfare system (John 6:25-40). The fearful disciples try to persuade him to avoid the cross (Mark 8:31-33). Yet, in each instance, Jesus refuses to compromise his principles or purpose. He expresses under this pressure a relentless focus on doing the work for which he was sent.

Grace in conflict and criticism. The Pharisees continually sought to trick Jesus into making statements or taking actions which, had he given in, would have hurt his influence with common people, opened him to arrest by the Romans or denied the kingdom values by which he lived (John 8:1-11; Matthew 22:15-22). The Jewish leaders repeatedly criticized him for his poor choice of companions (Mark 2:13-17), for his violation of religious norms (Mark 2:23-28), and for his claims to spiritual authority which they considered blasphemous (Luke 5:17-26). Yet, in all but a few cases, Jesus gave them not the tongue-lashing their blindness and hubris deserved, but gently sought to open their minds and hearts to the larger truth.

Grace in the face of foolishness. It is difficult for us to imagine the pressure placed on the patience of Jesus by the mere experience of walking with human beings. As Dallas Willard reminds us, Jesus was the most intelligent and morally sound person ever to walk the face of this earth.[1] His wisdom and goodness were so great that even the most gifted human beings would seem to be dressed in filthy rags (Isaiah 64:6) when compared to his splendor. What must it have been like for him to stand under the haughty scrutiny of Herod or Pilate, fancying themselves so powerful and bright? How did he who was the true King manage to treat them with the civility and humility he did (Luke 23:1-25; John 18:28-37)?

It was not just the ignorance of his enemies that might have rightly vexed Jesus. Even his closest disciples were hard-hearted toward others (Mark 6:30-36), consistently missed the point of his teachings (Mark 10:35-40; Luke 24:13-27), and were famously fickle in their faithfulness (Matthew 26:31-46). In the face of all the foolishness he met, Jesus kept expressing grace—enduring their slowness to learn, patiently redirecting them and forgiving their failures.

Grace in hardship and loss. Jesus lived the life of a traveling salesman. He felt the pangs of hunger and thirst and knew the weariness of walking long, hot miles. Jesus felt the sting of rejection, betrayal and abandonment, even by those closest to him. He wept hot tears over the death of those he loved. Jesus did not pretend life wasn't hard. He confessed that it was difficult to have no place to lay his head (Matthew 8:20). He let others see his tears of grief (John 11:35). He acknowledged his thirst (John 19:28) and feelings of forsakenness (Mark 15:34). And yet, in all these experiences there was never a hint of self-pity, no spirit of bitterness or indignant complaint. Even in his articulation of his suffering, Jesus expressed the character of grace.

THE SUPREME TEST

If you have ever stood at the bedside of someone who was dying, then you know how the prospect of imminent death has a way of surfacing someone's real substance. A person can go all through life wearing a veneer that conceals much of the true feelings and convictions that flow through the deep channels of his or her being. But when death presses upon a person, the true sap of that soul comes seeping out.

That is why the congregation that assembled at the foot of the cross probably waited with bated breath to hear what Jesus would say. The soldiers who had lashed him so savagely that the flesh hung in strips from his back must have waited for him to cry. The historian Seneca tells us that people who were crucified typically cursed the day they were born, the mother that bore them and certainly the executioners who sat beneath the gallows gambling for their clothes.[2]

Those who happened to pass by on the road to Jerusalem would have expected a cry of torment too. So awful would be the exchanges between those on the cross and passing hecklers that the Roman statesman Cicero informs us it was sometimes necessary to cut out the tongues of those who were crucified, just to stop the blasphemies and the volleys of bloody spit the dying criminals often rained down.[3]

Even the scribes and Pharisees—so eager to silence Jesus before—must have been eager to hear what he would say now. Surely he who had preached "Love your enemies [and] do good to those who hate you" (Luke 6:27) would now abandon that ridiculous gospel as the spikes sank into his flesh. Any resolution he had made to keep up appearances would, they surely thought, quickly dissolve as blood from the crown of thorns began to sting his eyes, as his exhausted limbs shrieked in pain, as his chest heaved in an agonized struggle for air. It would be very clear to all what this Nazarene carpenter truly was and was not.

> THE WORLD NEEDS TO SEE WHAT THE CHRISTIAN LIFE LOOKS LIKE. PEOPLE WHO THINK GOD IS UNNECESSARY, OR JUST OPTIONAL IN LIFE, NEED FRESH IMAGES OF HOW LIFE IS MEANT TO BE LIVED. THEY NEED HARD EVIDENCE THAT FOLLOWING JESUS REALLY MAKES A DIFFERENCE.
>
> Donald Posterski

THE AMAZING GRACE OF GOD

No human being was prepared for the message that came. No one save God could have predicted that the words would not be ones of punishment or pain, but rather of pardon. Jesus said: "Father, forgive them, for they do not know what they are doing" (Luke 23:34).

Unnatural. The first striking thing about the words Christ spoke on the cross is how unnatural they seem. It's just not natural for a victim to feel compassion for a victimizer. It's not natural to forgive the people who brazenly hurt, harass or malign you. How could Jesus forgive Caiaphas, the high priest, who allowed a soldier to strike him in the face with an armored fist? Or forgive Pilate, the gutless politician who would sentence to death a man he knows is innocent, just to protect his job? Forgive Herod, who would mock Wisdom by robing it in the clothes of a fool? Forgive Judas the backstabber, or Peter the windbag turncoat? Forgive the soldiers and the hecklers, when he had given so much for them and they now rejoiced in his pain? No. That kind of grace is simply unnatural.

Unconditional. What makes Christ's words on the cross even more amazing still is that the forgiveness he was extending was also *unconditional*. We would resonate with Jesus better if he had said, "Father, forgive them, as long as they take me down right now and bandage me up." If he had said: "Father, forgive them, as long as they apologize; or as long as they feel terrible about what they have done." This sort of forgiveness we understand, because it is the kind we often extend. But not Jesus. What he expresses under pressure is something else altogether. "Father, forgive them." No ifs, ands or buts.

Understanding. It is also important that we take in a third quality to the grace Jesus extends because it is this third quality that accounts for the first two. The deepest kind of forgiveness is unnatural and un-conditional precisely because it is *understanding*. What does Jesus understand? He understands that his murderers and mockers *don't*. They don't get it. "Father, forgive them, *for they know do not know what they do*." Reverend Fulton Sheen once wrote that if Christ's killers

knew what they were doing and still went on doing it; if they knew what a terrible crime they were committing by sentencing Life to death . . . they would never be saved! . . . In like manner, if we knew what a terrible thing sin was and went on sinning; if we knew how much love there was in the Sacrifice of the Cross and still refused to fill the chalice of our heart with that love; if we knew what gigantic failings God has overlooked in our case, but still continued judging others for their foibles . . . we should be utterly lost. It is not our wisdom that saves us; it is our colossal ignorance! It is only our ignorance of [how serious sin is and] how good God is that excuses us for not being saints.[4]

This, of course, is not an argument for deliberately remaining ignorant. It is, rather, an inspiration to become even more eager to repent of every vice and vanity in our lives, if only as a way of saying: "Thank you, Jesus, for what you did to save me when I was just too blind to see."

The amazing grace of Jesus ought, however, to have an even larger impact on us than that. Wouldn't you think it might dramatically increase the likelihood that we would express that kind of grace to someone else in a moment of pressure (Matthew 18:23-35)? When your marriage partner treats you coldly, or when your kids break your heart and hopes; when some slimy competitor or ungrateful customer rips you off; when a friend fails you in some painful way; when a salesclerk treats you rudely, or some slob steals your parking space, one of the greatest evidences that you have actually taken in the grace that God has expressed to you is that you will do more than simmer with anger, seal off your heart or plot some way of getting even. You will treat others like Jesus did you. As the hero in *Schindler's List* declares to his Nazi overseer: "Real power is when we have every justification to kill, and we don't." In other words, the greatest power of all is not the power to exact judgment but the power to pardon.

EXPRESS GRACE AT THE PRESSURE POINTS

Here's the bottom line: You may never go out on a professional basketball court or perform before a vast crowd elsewhere. Thanks to Jesus, you will not bear the weight he did upon the cross. But people notice your behavior. They are looking to see if you are any different than the other people they've met. Nothing you do will be a more convincing witness to the fact that you know Jesus than if they see you expressing grace when the pressure is on you. How can you do that? Seek to respond as Jesus did at the following common pressure-points of life.

Grace in the midst of temptation. The Bible says that Jesus is very able "to sympathize with our weaknesses" because he was "tempted in every way, just as we are—yet was without sin" (Hebrews 4:15). The message here is that temptation is one of the unavoidable pressures of life for us, just as it was for Jesus. It's not a sin to be tempted or even to feel somewhat weak in the face of it. Nondisciples will actually find us much more accessible if we can talk openly with them about the struggles we have with temptation, rather than trying to appear as if we never have an errant thought or troublesome urge.

There is a difference, however, between being momentarily tempted and actually leaning into it to the point where we're sinning. Jesus knew where the line was, and he can help us find it for ourselves. Nondisciples need to know that we're tempted, just as they are. But they also need to see that we're not giving in to every temptation that comes our way. The lives of Christ's witnesses have to be like "salt," said Jesus. If we aren't living in a way that is distinct from the world's rotting or bland morality, then we, like salt that has lost its saltiness, are "no longer good for anything, except to be thrown out and trampled" (Matthew 5:13).

Imagine you're out with friends and tempted to buy something you don't need. Suddenly, you catch yourself and say with a groan, "Oh, I'd really love to have that, but I think the money's going to mean a lot more to the kingdom investments I'm making." Or imagine that someone is dishing dirt on a fellow coworker who has applied for the same position you have. You could use this information to feel better about yourself or to increase your standing and power. But you check that temptation. "It's probably not good for me to know that or repeat it," you say. "I'm just as prone as anyone to wanting to go up by pulling other people down, but God is trying to change that in me, so I'm going to set that info aside."

Or suppose you're getting heaped with accolades for your performance at work or on the sports field. You instantly swell with pride, secretly feeling like your fans haven't said enough! But the figure of Jesus washing feet comes to your mind. "You know," you say, "it really feels great to be celebrated and to know I made a contribution. The worst part of me wants to take all the credit. But I know the gifts came from God and he definitely blessed me by making me part of this fabulous team." Imagine that you're sitting with an acquaintance and you notice an attractive person walking past your table. "There I go again," you say. "What?" your friend says. "It's fine to look if you don't touch." "That's what I always told myself," you respond. "But I

started thinking, *How would I feel if somebody treated my daughter like that? What's this habit doing to my affections for my own wife?* I began to see why Jesus told us to be very wary of lust."

People in this world are used to seeing others seeking fulfillment by satisfying all their physical appetites. They are accustomed to people who pursue power by any means. They know the pattern of those whose identity and security are staked in wowing the crowd. But when they see someone under these pressures expressing something different—displaying a greater health—some of them begin to wonder about this difference. They may even begin to ask why.

Grace in the face of diversion. Like Jesus, we also face the perpetual pressure to become diverted from the most important purposes of our life. Technology makes it possible to stay "in touch" with phenomenal numbers of people, but sometimes at the expense of the sustained conversations needed for deep relationships. The force of competition in the marketplace and the "need" to have the money to keep buying all the consumer "goods" everyone else seems to have can make longer hours at

> SEEKERS NEED TO SEE IN YOU MORE THAN DRY EYES AND PASTED-ON SMILES. THEY NEED TO SEE YOU GRAPPLE WITH FEAR AND SADNESS AND ANGER AND JEALOUSY AND LOSS. THEY NEED TO HEAR YOU TALK OPENLY ABOUT IT. THEY NEED TO WATCH YOU WORK OUT YOUR FAITH WITHOUT DISCOUNTING THE EVERYDAY EMOTIONAL REALITIES OF YOUR LIFE.
>
> Bill Hybels and Mark Mittelberg

work feel like a "necessity." The challenge, again, is that intimate relationships with family or friends, with God or our own heartbeat, can increasingly get pushed off our schedule. On top of this, we meet a constant parade of people who are eager to harness our energy, our reputation, our social network, our every resource to the wagon of their own ambitions and pre-occupations. "You must do this. You should do that. You simply can't say no." In this context, it is very easy to become diverted from our primary calling to love God and love people above all else.

Several years ago, I worked alongside a couple who seemed utterly out of step with the culture of our workplace. They limited their appointments to the number that allowed them to give full value to the people and tasks in front of them. When the demands on them clearly outstripped their gifts or capacity to manage them sanely, they would confess they needed help or ask for help to define a better way. On their days off, they actually stopped working. They didn't just talk about spiritual disciplines, but devoted hours to practicing them. They regularly disappointed people by limiting their social engagements in order to spend extended time with their most loved ones and people ready to get closer to God.

For a long time, I looked upon this pair as people with a "problem." They did not *get* the requirements of our culture. And then it slowly dawned on me: It was the culture that was the problem. This couple actually "got" the culture just fine. They

were simply making deliberate choices to try to live in a countercultural way. They were laboring to preserve a baseline of spiritual, physical and relational health of which many of us around them had simply lost sight.

As we saw earlier, Jesus was like this. He refused to become hostage to the expectations of his society, boldly declaring that his kingdom was not of this world (John 18:36). His primary purpose was to preserve his relationship with his Father and to pursue his mission of loving people into deeper relationships with him and with one another (Mark 12:28-31). Like all of us, Jesus got dragged off track now and then, but he always found his way back. There was a peace, power and beauty to Christ's life that expressed a gracious sanity he said he came to give to all of us. Seek this life with great intentionality, he said, because there are all kinds of forces arrayed to steal, kill and destroy it (John 10:10).

Strive to be like Jesus, and learn to live like the couple I've just described. No matter how hard it is to live counterculturally, work to be someone who displays to others what it looks like to live out of God's grace beneath the weight of this world's pressures.

Grace in conflict and criticism. I shared lunch with a remarkable disciple who had once been a high-ranking Communist Party official in Beijing. When I asked how he had come to faith, he told the story of watching the witness of Christian students during the notorious Tienanmen Square massacre of 1989. The courage of those believers, standing up to the government's tanks and guns and their refusal to take up violence to advance their cause, broke the heart of this atheist and convinced him of the power of God.

Over the years, I have heard many other stories of people whose spiritual turning point came as the result of watching the way certain Christian disciples have handled conflict and criticism. Few things soften hearts like seeing someone who, in spite of being brutally attacked, refuses to retaliate, who instead seeks to "overcome evil with good" (Romans 12:21). Every bit as impressive are disciples who actually welcome criticism. I've seen antagonists stumped speechless by a believer who humbly acknowledges when a critic has a very good point.

Lest this sound too romantic, let me be clear that criticism—particularly from aggressive or unhealthy people—is one of the most difficult pressures that any of us ever face. It is very hard not to become defensive, consumed with rationalizations, or respond by attacking the critical person. But what if we could do differently? When a nondisciple is rallying to your defense by demonizing your opponent, imagine saying, "Look, I really appreciate that you have my back. But what if this person is even partly right? If God is trying to say something to me through this person to help me grow, I definitely need to hear it." Or picture yourself opening up to some critic in your workplace or social circle and saying, "I understand you've got some issues with me. A big part of me wants to run from the conflict, but I've learned that sometimes it's Jesus using tough means to get my attention. Could you tell me more about what you feel I'm missing?"

The story is told that Abraham Lincoln was once sternly upbraided by a supporter for showing inordinate kindness toward a particularly vitriolic critic. "Why do you keep opening yourself to that person?" she allegedly asked. "Don't you realize that he is your sworn enemy? He's out to destroy you!" Lincoln is said to have calmly responded, "Yes, madam, but do I not destroy my enemy by making him my friend?" This is one of the reasons why Lincoln is remembered not only as one of America's greatest presidents but also one of the country's finest Christian witnesses. He expressed grace under pressure.

Grace in the face of foolishness. Not every critic bears the gift of wisdom. Like Jesus, we'll face our fair share of fools—at least as the world defines folly or worthlessness. We'll meet people who are unattractive in body or in spirit. We'll encounter those who are awkward, ill-informed, poor in cash or sullied by a dirty past. There is enormous social pressure in our world to ignore, avoid or disassociate ourselves from such people. All the gain seems to come from fraternizing with the bright, the brawny and the beautiful. But this, again, is why we need to remember Jesus. From his vantage point, none of us looked even remotely wise, worthy or winsome—"not even one" (Romans 3:10). Yet he loved us, came and gave his life for us, just the same (Romans 5:8).

Few things bear witness to the character of God and his kingdom as when, amidst the world's pressure to do otherwise, we express a loving grace to the unlovely and the ungraceful. What do nondisciples notice about the breadth of your compassion for such people? Does it reflect the care and courage by which the Son of God went in search of you and me?

Grace in hardship and loss. Finally, take seriously the opportunities for witness that come in the midst of your darkest hours. Within a year of becoming a follower of Jesus, my friend Bob saw the company he founded taken over by venture capitalists and his job eliminated. A few months later, his young wife died of breast cancer. He had no job, three grieving children and a hole in his heart the size of Texas. Everyone waited for Bob's faith to fold. It did just the opposite. His faith flowered. He grieved honestly and openly. He talked about the comfort he was finding in the arms of his church. He described his faith that his wife was enjoying life beyond the grave. He spoke to others of his belief that God would help him through this very hard time and one day bring great joy from great sorrow. In his darkest hour, Bob gave forth an incandescent witness that drew dozens closer to God.

Many of us hold a mistaken perception that people will be most drawn to Christ by seeing how many things are going *right* for us. Nondisciples typically take far greater notice of Christians when everything seems to be going wrong for us. It is when our heartstrings have snapped or our body is failing that they look to see what we do with what is left of our life. It is when we are being doubled-teamed by trial and tragedy that they pay attention to how we handle the ball.

A WATCHING WORLD

Will you handle temptation differently than others do? How will you deal with all that might divert you from your primary purpose? What will you do with conflict and criticism? How will you treat your enemies or those unlovely fools? What will you do when you're suffering much and losing a lot? Does the Christian faith make any difference in somebody's life when the pressure is really on? I pray that, somewhere, somebody is going to see grace pouring out of you, like it was expressed through Jesus. Let's live in such a way that some will say, "I'll never forget that I got to see one of Christ's great witnesses in action."

---

[1]Dallas Willard, *The Divine Conspiracy: Rediscovering Our Hidden Life in God* (San Francisco: HarperCollins, 1998), pp. 93-95.

[2]Seneca, *Dialogue* 6.20.3, "To Marcia on Consolation," in *Moral Essays*, trans. John W. Basore, The Loeb Classical Library (Cambridge, MA: Harvard University Press, 1946).

[3]Wenhua Shi, *Paul's Message of the Cross As Body Language*, trans. Mohr Siebeck (Tübingen, Germany: Laupp & Göbel, 2008), p. 31.

[4]Fulton J. Sheen, *The Seven Last Words* (Garden City, NY: Alba House, 1996), pp. 5-8.

Application Exercise

1. Who do you know that expresses grace under pressure and what have you particularly admired about this person?

2. What about the grace that Jesus showed under duress particularly impresses you?

3. Under which of the following pressures do you express a Christlike grace most consistently?

   ☐ In the midst of temptation

   ☐ In the face of diversion

   ☐ In conflict and criticism

   ☐ In the face of foolishness

   ☐ In hardship and loss

4. With which of these pressures do you need to develop greater capacity for gracious response? How might you go about handling this particular kind of pressure in a more gracious manner?

5. Complete this sentence: If I were to express greater grace under pressure in this area, others might notice that . . .

6. Does the reading convict, challenge or comfort you? Why?

Going Deeper

Aldrich, Joe. *Lifestyle Evangelism: Learning to Open Your Life to Those Around You.* Sisters, OR: Multnomah Publishers, 1993.

Yancey, Philip. *What's So Amazing About Grace?* Grand Rapids: Zondervan, 1997.

10 / Serve Needs

LOOKING AHEAD

Memory Verse: Matthew 5:13-16
Bible Study: Matthew 25:1-46
Reading: Love With Its Sleeves Rolled Up

 Core Truth

How can acts of service prepare the ground for people to want to receive the gospel we proclaim?

Many will be unwilling to consider the truth of the gospel until they experience proof of the love of Christ. We will spur newfound interest in the Christian message and life among hardened people only to the extent that our words are preceded or accompanied by Christ-like acts of service that address the felt needs of people where they are under pressure.

1. Identify key words or phrases in the question and answer above, and state their meaning in your own words.

2. Restate the core truth in your own words.

3. What questions or issues does the core truth raise for you?

Memory Verse Study Guide

Copy the entire text here:

_____

_____

_____

_____

_____

_____

_____

_____

_____

_____

_____

_____

_____

_____

_____

_____

_____

_____

_____

_____

Memory Verse: Matthew 5:13-16

Jesus made it clear that his disciples were meant to exert a catalytic influence upon the world around them. In this passage, he provides us with two word pictures that help to describe the nature of this calling.

1. *Putting it in context:* Our memory verse is found within Christ's famous Sermon on the Mount (Matthew 5–7), a rich discourse in which Jesus describes the blessed way of living he intends for his disciples. *Read Matthew 5:1-12.* How does this picture compare with the way most people think of the good life?

2. *Read Matthew 5:13.* List below the different functions you associate with salt.

3. In what ways could acts of service to others function in a similar way?

4. What does it mean to lose our saltiness?

5. *Read Matthew 5:14-15.* Describe the effect of light in the two instances that Jesus cites in these verses?

a. A city on a hill:

b. A lamp:

6. How might Christians serving others have a similar "lighting" effect?

7. *Read Matthew 5:16.* What does Jesus say is the desired result of our good deeds?

Inductive Bible Study Guide

Bible Study: Matthew 25:1-46

One of the great themes of the New Testament is the importance of preparedness. As we explored in chapter seven, Christ's disciples are called to "always be prepared to give an answer" for the hope that they have (1 Peter 3:15). In this passage, Jesus tells three parables aimed at describing some of the other kinds of readiness needed in the lives of his disciples.

1. *Read Matthew 25:1-13*. What is the crucial difference between the five virgins who are ready for the bridegroom's return and the five who are not?

2. Given the importance that Jesus assigned to shedding light (see, for example, Matthew 5:14-16), what might the oil in this story represent (Matthew 25:3, 8-10)?

3. *Read Matthew 25:14-30*. In this parable, Jesus tells the story of a master who entrusts the care of his resources to three servants. What is the difference between the behavior of the two that are rewarded and the one who is cast out when the master suddenly returns from his journey?

4. What is Jesus saying we must be ready to do with the resources he has given us?

5. *Read Matthew 25:31-46.* This third parable builds on the previous two. On the basis of what behavior does the King separate the blessed sheep from the accursed goats?

6. How would you describe the importance Jesus assigns to investing ourselves in acts of service that extend the life of his kingdom to others?

7. What questions or issues does this passage raise for you?

Reading: Love with Its Sleeves Rolled Up

WHEN OTHERS ARE UNDER PRESSURE

When the tsunami wave hit the coast of Sri Lanka on December 26, 2004, the lives of 30,000 precious souls were lost in a matter of minutes. In the Kalutara region alone, 4,000 houses were washed away in an instant, leaving 14,000 people homeless. Survivors wandered through the wreckage, lost in grief, confusion and despair.

Not everyone was stunned into a stupor. When A. D. Karunarathna, the principal of the nearby St. John's Christian School, heard the early reports, his response was immediate action. Aware that his school stood on high dry ground, he issued an order to his staff: "Open the gates," he said. "Open all the doors. Let everyone in."

Previously, the primarily Muslim and Buddhist residents of Kalutara had looked upon that Christian school with a mixture of hostility, suspicion and apathy. In the first ten days after the tsunami, however, more than 2,200 refugees streamed through the gates of St. John's. The school staff turned their normally orderly classrooms into dormitories. They converted their polished banisters and desks into drying stations for clothes. They set up outhouses and a medical treatment center. They gave haircuts and fed people.

> I HAVE NEVER HEARD ANYTHING ABOUT THE RESOLUTIONS OF THE APOSTLES, BUT A GREAT DEAL ABOUT THEIR ACTS.
>
> Horace Mann

"I decided we had to do everything we could for people," said Karunarathna. "We had to treat them with respect [and] listen to them."[1]

Do you suppose the people of Kalutara are now feeling more respect for the people of St. John's Christian School? Are any of them more inclined today to listen to what the Christian disciples there have to say about their gospel? It seems likely that the answer is yes. The only witness more effective than disciples who express grace when *they* are under pressure is when those same disciples exhibit love with its sleeves rolled up to others in *their* moments of profound duress.

THE PROOF OF THE TRUTH

Not since the first century has this form of witness been more essential to the spread of the gospel's influence. There is widespread interest in spirituality but great difference of opinion as to which religious convictions offer the most help or hope. There is a prevailing skepticism about the truth claims of any one religion and outright cynicism about the value of organized religion in general. If we are going to reach the people of this world in significantly greater numbers, then alongside our verbal testimony, our humble nailing of our own sin, and our display of God's grace when we are pressed, we also need this fourth form of witness—a lifestyle of servanthood that authenticates the gospel we proclaim. Robert Lewis makes the case as follows:

> The church often lacks the credibility necessary for our age. We continue in our attempt to blindly build bridges to our world solely on a disembodied truth model. But to our age, truth is nothing more than talk. . . . Our postmodern world is tired of words—it wants *real*. Real is everything. Real is convincing. And yet, real is something the church seems less and less geared to demonstrating, much less producing. What we *are* geared to is slicker, more technologically brilliant presentations of truth. But . . . where is the love of God we talk about? Where is the transforming power of Christ? The changed lives? The selfless giving? The good works?[2]

Lewis goes on to beg believers to see the futility of trying to fulfill the Great Commission to *go* (Matthew 28:18-20) without first living out the Great Commandment to *love* (Matthew 22:36-39). Especially in this "new first century," words of truth will be very slow to take root on ground that has not first been plowed up and prepared by works of love. This is why the message of contemporary Christianity often falls on deaf ears. We have too often tried to give people cognitive truth without first extending to them the convincing proof of our gospel that comes through an experience of God's self-giving love.

The Servant of All

There were a lot of impoverished people in Christ's day, as there are in ours. These people were accustomed to getting occasional alms or prayer from the pious or privileged members of society. Sadly, those with resources did not always follow through. This is why the ministry of Jesus created such a dramatic stir. Before he ever asked people to serve God, he made it clear that he came to serve them. "The Son of Man," Jesus said, "came not to be served, but to serve." And then, in a myriad of practical ways, Jesus showed the world what true greatness looks like in the life of one willing to be "the servant of all" (Mark 9:33-35).

Needs that Christ met. The Bible teaches that Jesus, in the course of drawing sinners to himself, also met many of their nonspiritual needs as well. For instance, he met *medical needs* through physically healing the afflicted (Matthew 4:23). He served people's *dietary needs* by feeding thousands (Matthew 14:15-21). He served their *hygienic needs* by stooping to wash filthy feet (John 13:3-17). He served *legal needs* by standing between people and their accusers (John 8:1-11). Jesus served

> I DECIDED TO MAKE MY LIFE MY
>
> ARGUMENT.
>
> Albert Schweitzer

people's *educational needs* by forming a traveling school in which even fishermen, tax collectors and prostitutes could enroll (Matthew 4:19; 9:9; Luke 8:1-3). He served the *physical and emotional needs* of those he met by lifting burdens and taking them to places where they could rest (Matthew 11:28-29; Mark 6:31). He addressed people's *social needs* by demonstrating the worth of outcasts and people lost in the crowd (John 4:1-26; Luke 19:1-6). Even when he was hanging on a cross in agony, Jesus kept on serving. He served the *family needs* of Mary and John by giving one an adopted son and the other a new mother (John 19:25-27). He served the *eternal needs* of a repentant thief by assuring him a place in paradise (Luke 23:39-43). And Jesus served the *spiritual needs* of all of us by paying our debt on the cross (Mark 10:45; John 19:30).

Signs of the kingdom. So deep and expansive was the service of Jesus to human need that the apostle John gave these actions a special name. He called them *semeia*—literally, "signs."[3] These servant actions were proof of the truth that at the core of this universe is not a silent, insensible emptiness, but rather a thundering heartbeat—a life-changing Love committed to the salvation of human life at every level (Romans 1:16).

Christ's call to his disciples. Jesus made it clear that anyone who really knew him would move toward others in a similarly servant-hearted way (Matthew 7:21-23). He went so far as to say that to fail to supply the needs of the hungry and thirsty, or to neglect hospitality toward a stranger, or to refuse to offer care for the needs of the cold, sick or imprisoned person was evidence of nondiscipleship and grounds for dismissal from his company (Matthew 25:31-46). Jesus expected his followers to be like their master (Matthew 10:25) in their servant love. He believed that the good deeds his disciples performed in their efforts to meet the needs of others would be one of the primary ways that they displayed a distinctiveness (like salt) and a radiance (like light) that would result in other people being drawn to their Father in heaven (Matthew 5:13-16).

The servant witness of the early church. Christ's first disciples obviously took this commission very seriously. As sociologist Rodney Stark has described, the early Christians tended the sick and dying and took widows and orphans under their wings. They fed the hungry, welcomed aliens and strangers, advocated for women and slaves, protected children and cared for prisoners. In a legion of ways they gave practical proof of the spiritual truth they professed. Stark concluded that the church's way of life was so effective in improving the condition of humanity and so attractive in its spirit of service and hope that it won the hearts of millions in a world that had become largely dead to organized religion.[4] The Bible tells the story this way:

> All the believers were one in heart and mind. No one claimed that any of their possessions was their own, but they shared everything they had.

. . . There were no needy persons among them. (Acts 4:32-34 TNIV)

Everyone was filled with awe at the many wonders and signs performed by the apostles. . . . They sold property and possessions to give to anyone who had need . . . praising God and enjoying the favor of all the people. And the Lord added to their number daily those who were being saved. (Acts 2:43-47 TNIV)

WHAT SERVANTHOOD IS AND ISN'T

How might this happen again? How could Christian disciples today become people whose lifestyle is so obviously life-giving that we inspire "the favor of all the people" and move others to ask, "How do I get in on what you people have and know?" The answer is the same as the one once given to a man who was speaking eloquently to his wife about how much he loved her. "I love you so much," he said, "I would even die for you." "That won't be necessary," his wife responded. "Just roll up your sleeves, pick up that towel and help me with the dishes."

How many times has Jesus longed to see that kind of simple devotion in his disciples? Maybe you are someone who has already taken up a towel in service to others, as Jesus did (John 13:1-17). The truth is that we sometimes get confused about

> JESUS GAVE US A NEW NORM OF GREATNESS. HE WHO IS GREATEST AMONG YOU SHALL BE YOUR SERVANT. YOU ONLY NEED A HEART FULL OF GRACE, A SOUL GENERATED BY LOVE.
>
> Martin Luther King Jr.

the nature of servanthood. Unless it is done in the same Spirit with which Jesus served, our service to others can easily become the slave of impulses that do not fulfill the purposes of God. Several important distinctions are worth considering here.

An opportunity, not an obligation. Sometimes people speak or behave as if serving others were a distasteful duty—like eating broccoli, doing homework or paying taxes. This, however, is not the attitude with which Jesus served. The Bible says that it was "for the joy set before him" that Jesus performed his service to people (Hebrews 12:2). This doesn't mean that for Jesus service was always pleasant or easy. There's not a whole lot about washing dirty feet or taking up a cross which fits that description. But joy is much greater than happiness with the volume turned up and it is rarely attained easily. Jesus said that the "the kingdom of heaven is like treasure hidden in a field. When a man found it, he hid it again, and then in his joy went and sold all he had and bought that field" (Matthew 13:44). Jesus understood that there were costs to gaining the kingdom, but he regarded the opportunity to do the Father's will as an act of joy. When he invited his disciples to come take part in kingdom work, he wasn't laying an obligation on us but offering an opportunity to us—to let our lives be caught up in the magnificent movement of God's redeeming grace.

A response, not a racket. Other times, service becomes just another one of those rackets people set up to feel better about themselves, earn the admiration of others or reap a tax deduction. "Check out all my volunteer and charitable activities. Look at how creative, hardworking or sacrificial I am!" Here, again, this isn't even close to servanthood in the Jesus sense. Christ explicitly cautioned his followers not to be like the hypocrites who announce their gifts to the needy with trumpets "to be honored by men." He expected his disciples to be people who routinely served other people in secret, content that God alone knew what they were doing (Matthew 6:1-4). He believed that we'd give to others not out of a desire for glory but as a response of gratitude for all that God has given us.

An act of communion, not condescension. There are also some who feel that serving others is an act of noblesse oblige. Though they may never say it aloud, their thinking is: *I have so much; the noble thing is to share with this person who doesn't. I'm a charitable giver; this other person is a fortunate receiver.* The truth, however, is that none of us are truly self-made, self-continuing or self-fulfilling. As any severe illness, disaster or crisis quickly reminds us, we are all dependent creatures. The poorest widow we meet may have riches of spirit or insight without which we are impoverished (Mark 12:41-44). How many of us, when serving the poor, have found ourselves served in ways we never expected? This is why serving somebody else is not an act of condescension but actually one of communion. It is one of those moments when we bear witness to the fact that all of us are paupers, desperately in need of the grace of God and the gifts that others can offer us.

A gift, not a guarantee. In most human relationships we learn that gifts often come with strings attached. "I will scratch your back, so long as you scratch mine. I'll do the laundry, if you'll take out the garbage." Some of this is the reciprocity of healthy relationship. If we are not careful, however, the contributions we make can start to feel like rightful claims on the behavior of others. How many of us have done acts of apparent "service" while expecting to be thanked for our work or to see the other person change their behavior in a way that pleases us? As understandable as this is, it isn't servanthood as Jesus defined it for his disciples:

> If you love those who love you, what credit is that to you? Even sinners love those who love them. And if you do good to those who are good to you, what credit is that to you? Even sinners do that. And if you lend to those from whom you expect repayment, what credit is that to you? Even sinners lend to sinners, expecting to be repaid in full. But love your enemies, do good to them, and lend to them without expecting to get anything back. Then your reward

will be great, and you will be children of the Most High, because he is kind to the ungrateful and wicked. (Luke 6:32-35 TNIV)

If we are to serve as Jesus served, then it has to be a gift with no guarantee of return, except for the knowledge that we have in some small measure extended the kind of grace which God gives us.

A statement, not a strategy. All of these characteristics of servanthood converge in one final distinction that can easily be missed. To put it bluntly, sometimes well-meaning Christians will serve others as an evangelism strategy. They'll extend "kindness" to neighbors as a means of priming them for spiritual conquest. They'll sponsor free car washes or offer free lunches as a premise for passing along Christian literature. They may even hold a community service day, hoping that the sight of matching T-shirts and cheerily done deeds will make people want to come out to their church.

When we look closely at the times when Jesus fed, healed or otherwise helped people, you will see that there was never a hint of marketing or manipulation in his acts. When he did good for people, he did it for one reason alone—to make a statement as simple as this: "God loves you." Whether you follow me or not, whether you thank me or not, whether you do good to me or not, whether you listen to me or not, this is still the fact: I love you.

A different kind of servant. If we are going to be Christlike witnesses in our time, then our serving needs to be like this. People have to sense that we serve them not out of obligation but with a spirit of joyful opportunity. They need to be clear that it's not just another racket we use to feel better about ourselves or earn their affirmation but a grateful response to the way we've been served by God. People must be able to discern that they are meeting in us not condescension but a genuine desire for communion with them. They need to know that what we offer is an open-handed gift, not a covert attempt to wrangle some kind of guarantee from them. They may not fully understand it at first but, in time, they will come to sense that what we are doing isn't a secret strategy but a sincere statement: They are genuinely loved by God (John 3:16-17).

GET A RINGSIDE SEAT AT MIRACLES
A man in our church has spent untold hours over the past fifty years visiting kids locked away in the juvenile detention centers of some of our nation's toughest cities. He extends the hand of friendship to them at a time when no other hand is there. "Why do you do this?" he is frequently asked. "The failure rate is high. Why don't you invest your energies someplace else?" The man's face spreads into a smile. "I keep going back because, now and then, I see the love of Christ take hold of a life and really turn it around. God has given me *a ringside seat at miracles.*"

Have you ever been so close to a miracle that you felt like you had a ringside seat?

Have you considered to whom you might devote your time in service of the Lord? It might be your calling to visit prisoners, or join a mission organization, or volunteer with a nonprofit venture that gives assistance to the poor. Perhaps, however, God wants to use you to serve needs in some other way. Here are a few ideas to spur you on (Hebrews 10:24).

Start a kingdom conspiracy. More than a decade ago now, a homemaker in our congregation was moved by the thought of so much money going to unnecessary Christmas presents while the basic needs of people around the world were unmet. Carol started an alternative Christmas market called Spirit Village that offers people the opportunity to purchase small items that make a large difference in the lives of the very poor. Instead of buying Uncle Al another necktie he doesn't really need, he might instead receive a Christmas card with a note inside that says: "In your name, five chickens were purchased for a needy family in Ethiopia." In the past ten years, some $1.5 million worth of livestock, educational resources, medical supplies, leadership training and more has been contributed through Spirit Village to people who really need assistance.

A few disciples in our area have banded together to provide a bridge into mainstream life for homeless single mothers or the impoverished women they met at a local food pantry. They now marvel at how the relationships they've formed have met deep needs for mentoring and learning on both sides. Not long ago, a group of disciples from our church was moved with compassion for the needs of the solitary elderly and their fatigued caregivers. Drawing together a band of nurses, doctors, social workers, lawyers and other volunteers, they formed a ministry called ASK (Advocacy, Support, Knowledge) that provides resources to people dealing with the challenges of aging. People will call in and inquire, "I've heard about the service you offer, but I need to tell you that I'm not a member of your church. Do I need to join to get help?" "No," the ASK workers respond. "*We* joined so that *you* could have help. Tell us about your need."

Pray for people in their presence. One of the most underserved needs of people in this world is for someone to bring their deep concerns before God. Sometimes, it is impossible to change their circumstances, but if you can let them know that someone truly cares enough to treat their needs as important enough to bring before God, it may ease their burden or perhaps even change their perception of God. When someone shares with you a worry or burden, ask them if you can pray on their behalf right now. If they say no, respect that and pray for their concern when you're on your own. More often than not, however, you'll find that they say yes. Bow your head and offer a very brief prayer along the following lines: "God, I know that you are very aware of the burden that _____ is carrying right now. Please pour out your grace upon this need. Help _____ to feel your love coming close to him/her. In

Jesus' name. Amen." Ask about that concern the next time you are with that person.

Brighten up a common place. I meet with a small group for study and prayer at a coffee shop next to a train station. It's a place where you readily feel the speed and pressure of people's lives today. One morning, we arranged with the hostess to cover the cost of whatever anyone ordered during the time our group met. As she handed them their coffee or breakfast, each commuter would pull out a wallet to pay, but the hostess would say: "That's OK, it's been covered." It was a study in how various people respond to grace. A few people just shrugged and walked away. A couple of people insisted on paying for themselves. Most people, however, seemed very pleasantly surprised and the tension on their faces lifted. Only if they really pressed her would the hostess tell them, "It's on the guys in the corner." We (the "guys in the corner") didn't do this to be thanked or noticed. It did, however, lead to a few great conversations with people curious about our motivation.

Be a secret desperado. I like even better the kind of servanthood practiced by a group of disciples at a church in Seattle. These people would hear of someone's need, meet it and simply leave a note behind that said: "You are loved and prayed for. Signed, God's Desperadoes." The beauty of this was threefold. Someone got a bag of groceries or a big bill covered at a time of great need. God got the credit. And, unexpectedly, the circle of desperadoes grew as more and more people, many of them formerly non-Christians, learned of this movement of love and realized what joy there would be in joining it.

Practice workplace chaplaincy. Carl was a senior executive of a major company at the time of a corporate merger. He was assigned the task of laying off a hundred of his colleagues, then turning out the lights himself. The prospect was devastating. He knew that many of these people had bills they were already struggling to pay, marriages that were already fragile and slim prospects of landing on their feet quickly. It dawned on him, however, that maybe God's purpose in putting him in this position was so that he could be an agent of grace at just such a time (Esther 4:14). In the weeks that followed, Carl went to bat for each of his employees—arguing for better severance arrangements, arranging new placements where possible and simply weeping with others in their time of need. At the end of the process, the people he'd fired threw a surprise party for him. Someone said that day: "Carl, we knew that your faith was important to *you*. What we didn't know until all of this happened was how important your faith would be to *us*." What are the needs of the people in your workplace? How could you pick up a towel to serve them?

Come alongside the wounded. It is amazing how even the most painful struggles and scars a disciple endures can be employed by Jesus to extend his witness. I've known many people who have experienced severe illness, the loss of a child, unemployment, marital turmoil, divorce or addiction. While they would never choose to endure those trials again, many confessed that it was these unwanted trials that God mysteriously used to help them build a redemptive relationship with someone in similar need. What are the hurts and hurdles you've face in life? How might they have prepared you to serve someone in need?

Open your heart and home. Richard Meyer tells the story of an elderly woman who heard a sermon in which she felt God encouraging her to look for ways in which she could use her particular gifts and situation to minister to the needs of others. She thought about her gifts and realized that she'd been told by others that she had the gift of hospitality. She lived alone in a small apartment near a large university and had afternoons free. She pondered the needs around her and the people who tugged at her heartstrings. To her mind came the students nearby who were so far away from home. It was then that an idea both strange and simple suddenly arose. She got a stack of three-by-five cards and wrote on each one the following words: "Are you homesick? Come to my house at 4:00 p.m. for tea." She included a phone number and address and then posted the cards all around campus. After a slow start, homesick students began trickling into her house each week for tea. When she died ten years later, eighty honorary pallbearers attended her funeral. Each one of them had been a student who, once upon a time, found a hot cup of tea, a sense of home and the gospel of Jesus in the hospitable heart of this faithful servant.

THE WHOLE GOSPEL

So what are *your* gifts? What's your situation? What are the needs around you? And how long do you think it would take for a lot more people to become intrigued with Christ and his church if even half of us resolved afresh to demonstrate love with its sleeves rolled up?

In his marvelous book, *The Hole in Our Gospel*, Richard Stearns ponders what might happen to the credibility and influence of the Christian movement if our Lord's disciples got even half-serious about using what God has entrusted to them to really serve the world's needs.

> Picture a different world. Imagine one in which two billion Christians embrace the whole gospel. . . . Visualize armies of compassion stationed in every corner of our world, doing small things with great love. . . . Might the world take notice? Would they ask new questions? Who are these people so motivated by love? Where did they come from? Why do they sacrifice so to help those the world has forgotten? Where do they find their strength? Who is this God they serve?[5]

So let's open the gates, like those disciples from Kalutara did. Let's offer to people the proof of the truth that there is a God whose love and grace is greater than the tsunamis of need that batter the shorelines of the world. If we do this, the Lord will begin adding daily to the number of those being saved (Acts 2:47).

---

[1]Kim Barker, "Sri Lankans Who Lost All Find Friendship at Shelter," *Chicago Tribune*, January 3, 2005.

[2]Robert Lewis, *The Church of Irresistible Influence* (Grand Rapids: Zondervan, 2001), pp. 40-41.

[3]See, for example, John 2:11, 18, 23; 3:2; 4:54; 6:2, 14, 26; 7:31; 9:16; 10:41; 11:47; 12:18, 37; 20:30; Revelation 12:1, 3; 13:13-14; 15:1; 16:14; 19:20.

[4]Rodney Stark, *The Rise of Christianity: A Sociologist Reconsiders History* (Princeton, NJ: Princeton University Press, 1996).

[5]Richard Stearns, *The Hole in Our Gospel* (Nashville: Thomas Nelson, 2009), pp. 278-79.

Application Exercise

1. List some of the practical needs of nondisciples within your reach.

2. Describe an act of Christlike service in response to one of the needs you listed above that could help provide "proof of the truth" that our Lord is a God of life-changing love.

3. The reading made some distinctions between the orientation toward servanthood modeled by Jesus and the distorted approaches to serving others common in our day. Which of the distorted approaches would you confess to practicing at times?

   ☐ Serving out of a sense of obligation vs. opportunity

   ☐ Using service as a selfish racket vs. a grateful response

   ☐ Serving as an act of condescension vs. communion

   ☐ Offering service to guarantee response vs. offering a gift

   ☐ Serving as an outreach strategy vs. a statement of love

4. Of the various examples of service described in the reading, which touched or inspired you and why?

5. What could you imagine happening if more of the disciples in your circle of acquaintance became extremely committed to being salt and light, investors of talents, and ministers of grace to "the least of these" in your community?

6. Does the reading convict, challenge or comfort you? Why?

Going Deeper

Lewis, Robert. *The Church of Irresistible Influence: Bridge-Building Stories to Help Reach Your Community*. Grand Rapids: Zondervan, 2001.

Ogden, Greg, and Daniel Meyer. *Leadership Essentials: Shaping Vision, Multiplying Influence, Defining Character*. Downers Grove, IL: InterVarsity Press, 2007.

Rusaw, Rick, and Eric Swanson. *The Externally-Focused Church*. Loveland, CO: Group, 2004.

Sider, Ronald J., Philip N. Olson and Heidi Bolland Unruh. *Churches That Make a Difference: Reaching Your Community with Good News and Good Works*. Grand Rapids: Baker Books, 2002.

Stearns, Richard. *The Hole in Our Gospel*. Nashville: Thomas Nelson, 2009.

Part Four

HELPING SOMEONE HOME

Before introducing what we'll be covering in this section, let's take a moment to review the path we've been traveling together over the course of this book.

Part One: Seeing the Big Picture: You know that Jesus calls you to join the great cloud of witnesses who have brought the good news of salvation to this world God so loves (*chap. 1*). You've examined the message of the gospel carefully and can see that it involves salvation in more ways than many people typically think (*chap. 2*). Since being a witness in our age comes with some particular challenges, you've also considered the changed conditions in our time and how mourning and moving through these opens us to the wonderful opportunities of this "new first century" (*chap. 3*).

Part Two: Reaching Out to People: Because you want to pursue your calling in the spirit of Jesus, you know how important it is for you to be filled with God's yearning heart for people *(chap. 4)*. You've also reflected on what it looks like to walk in love with people out in the world as Jesus did *(chap. 5)*. From this context, you've begun to investigate the soil of others' lives so that fruitful spiritual conversations with them can begin to unfold in a natural way *(chap. 6)*.

Part Three: Displaying Christ in You: By now, you have also been reminded that nothing so increases the credibility and attractiveness of the gospel message as seeing its effects in the life of a disciple. You are clear on how important it is for you to testify to the truth you know about God *(chap. 7)* and to nail the sin in your life honestly and openly *(chap. 8)*. You understand the impact you can have as nondisciples see how you express grace under pressure *(chap. 9)* and serve people's needs in a Christlike way *(chap. 10)*.

Now it is time to consider how you can perform the two most essential acts of Christian witness. Everything we've talked about so far has been aimed at preparing you for these final two movements by which you help someone home to the life of God.

Part Four: Share the Invitation to Salvation (chap. 11). At the end of the day, every Christian witness hopes to help someone say yes to beginning a new life with Christ. In this chapter we'll consider the power of invitation and learn from the style of Jesus. We'll then examine some specific questions you can ask nondisciples in order to assist them across the line of decision into a personal relationship with Jesus Christ.

Point Out the Pathway (chap. 12). Lastly, we'll look at the "great imperatives" that must be the final exclamation marks in the work of a witness. It is a magnificent privilege to lead someone to Christ. For this relationship to be all that it can be, however, we need to lead people past the point of decision and into the intentional journey of discipleship. What that life involves is the focus of this final chapter and the start of the next adventure.

11 / Share the Invitation to Salvation

MEMORY VERSE: Revelation 3:20
BIBLE STUDY: John 1:35-51
READING: Getting to Yes

 Core Truth

How can we share the invitation to salvation in a way more likely to yield an authentic and life-changing YES from others?

Recognizing the resistance some people have to Christianity and spiritual commitment, we need to invite others toward God in the way modeled by Jesus. When the Holy Spirit instructs us that someone may be ready to take the most essential step of faith, we can ask several commitment-advancing questions that may lead them across the line of decision into a saving relationship with Jesus Christ.

1. Identify key words or phrases in the question and answer above, and state their meaning in your own words.

2. Restate the core truth in your own words.

3. What questions or issues does the core truth raise for you?

Memory Verse Study Guide

Copy the entire text here:

_____

_____

_____

_____

_____

_____

_____

_____

_____

_____

_____

_____

_____

_____

_____

_____

_____

_____

_____

_____

Memory Verse: Revelation 3:20

The book of Revelation is jam-packed with vivid images of the person of Jesus. He is presented as a lion, a lamb, a shepherd, a reigning king and more. Few pictures of Christ are as instructive to the ministry of his witnesses, however, as the one found in the third chapter of Revelation. We meet him here as the Great Inviter.

1. *Putting it in context:* Our memory verse is set within Christ's letter to the church at Laodicea. Read Revelation 3:14-19. What does Jesus criticize or challenge?

2. Jesus is addressing the church in this letter, but how is the spiritual condition of the Laodiceans similar to those who have not made a commitment to being a disciple?

3. *Read Revelation 3:20.* Describe the picture of Jesus given in this verse. Where is he standing and what is he doing?

4. What do you think the "door" represents?

5. What is significant about the fact that Christ stands *outside* the door and that he *knocks*? Why are these two things significant?

6. What will be the outcome of someone opening the door and what is the significance of that image?

7. How have these verses spoken to you?

Inductive Bible Study Guide

Bible Study: John 1:35-51

In this passage we are reminded again how much people's spiritual progress depends upon the invitations that others issue to them. God draws people to himself through those willing to provide verbal entrance ramps to others.

1. *Read John 1:35-51.* List below all of the invitations recorded in this passage.

2. What does John the Baptizer invite people to do and why is this particular invitation important to our work as witnesses (vv. 35-36)?

3. What does Jesus invite John's two followers to tell him and why might this question be a helpful one for us to ask others (vv. 37-38)?

4. What is the subsequent invitation Jesus issues and what does it tell us about how people develop an understanding of Jesus and his Way (v. 39)?

5. What is the resistance that Nathanael has to meeting Jesus and how does Philip respond to it (v. 46)?

6. What does Jesus' interaction with Nathanael suggest to you about God's heart and vision for people (vv. 47-51)?

7. What questions or issues does this passage raise for you?

Reading: Getting to *Yes*

THE POWER OF AN INVITATION

Many years ago, two friends invited me to go on a double-date with them and a young woman one of them knew. As politely as I could, I turned down their invitations on numerous occasions. The couple, however, persisted. To end the assault, I finally gave in and consented to go with them. It turned out that my blind date had put up a similar fight and had also surrendered. Both of us showed up, gritting our teeth, praying for the endurance to get through the evening. It was March 21. On December 31 of that same year we were happily married!

How many life-changing experiences depend upon an invitation? I think of the men who dragged me into the game of golf, or the friend who took me to my first rock concert, or the one who introduced me to the pleasure of Indian food. My life has been profoundly enriched by people who took the initiative—sometimes repeatedly and without early success—to invite me into an experience I was reluctant or outright resistant to entering on my own.

You can probably think of similar stories from your own life. The point is that there are glories we will miss altogether unless someone issues an invitation. How you can go about sharing with others the greatest invitation of all is the thrust of this whole book and the special focus of this chapter. Let's bring together all the streams of thought we've been studying and see how they meet at this crucial point of invitation.

THE NAZARETH SYNDROME

In John's gospel, we read of a conversation between one of the very first disciples, Philip, and a man named Nathanael. Philip tells his friend that he's found in the person of Jesus of Nazareth the answer to his long-held longings for a greater life for himself and Israel. Philip hopes that Nathanael will respond with warm curiosity. Yet Nathanael's response is very different. "Nazareth!?" he exclaims. "Can anything good come from there?" (John 1:46).

To fully appreciate the meaning of this statement and its relevance for our own ministry requires a bit of background. Nazareth was the town the Romans had chosen to house their garrison for the northern regions of Israel. The city was teeming with Roman soldiers. The citizens there made a living by providing goods and services to the Roman soldiers who occupied their city. Most other Jews avoided entering that city if they could help it. The town had become associated with conquest, control and regulations.

> OF COURSE PEOPLE WITH PIERCED BODY PARTS ARE WELCOME IN OUR CHURCH.
>
> Words written on a church poster depicting the crucifixion

No wonder Nathanael was skeptical about meeting someone from there.

As we've explored in this book, it is sobering to realize that the word *church* has come to represent a place with a similarly poor reputation. Like Nazareth of old, part of the problem is some of the people who have occupied it. There are many fabulous people here, but there are also those with tongues as sharp as any Roman spear. There are some who have armored themselves up with self-righteousness and others who seem bent on conquering others or enforcing a set of rules. There are church officers who have used their power abusively. There are churchgoers who seem blind to their compromise and hypocrisy. There are those who seem clueless as to why everyone wouldn't want immediately to adopt all the costumes and rituals of their religious army. This is why when we say, "Would you like to come to church with me?" some nondisciples react as if we've said, "Would you like to come to my dentist with me?"

LEARN FROM JESUS' STYLE OF INVITATION

Obviously, if we are going to overcome the Nazareth Syndrome, then we need to rethink how we go about inviting people into the life of the kingdom of God. Throughout this book, we've been examining a variety of ways through which we can prepare the ground for a better response from nondisciples than the one Philip initially got from Nathanael. Coming full circle, let's see what we can learn from the style that Jesus employed when inviting people closer to him and his Father's kingdom. Five specific elements are worth noting.

1. Be progressive. When we study the approach Jesus took to exerting a transforming influence on others, the first element we notice is the progressive nature of his invitations. Unless the person came to him in an obvious state of readiness for deep investment in him, Jesus almost always started by inviting further engagement at a very nonthreatening level: "Come to me," he said. "Come dine with me." "Come fish with me." As he established a relationship of trust with someone, Jesus then turned up the intensity of his invitations a click or two: "Come follow me," he entreated. "Come learn from me. Come serve with me." It was only when the relationship was strong and he sensed the other person's readiness to take a further step that Jesus turned the dial of invitation further still: "Come live for me. Come die to yourself with me. Come let me live in you." The ministry of Jesus included issuing progressively deeper and more demanding invitations, based on the readiness of the other to say yes.

Our process of inviting others into the life of the kingdom of God needs to display this sensitivity too. It is possible that you'll talk tomorrow with some nonreligious person who would respond well if you invited them to confess their need of a Savior and commit their lives entirely to the lordship of Jesus Christ. But it is more likely that what would work even better is if you invited them out for coffee to talk about what's going on in their life. Eventually, you might invite them to dinner so that you could introduce them to other disciples. Further along, you might invite them to share with you what their experience of spirituality or religion has been and just listen, seeking to understand what excites or troubles them. At an appropriate time, you might invite them to attend with you a special event or worship service where they can experience how God is active through the church and his people.

At each step, invite those to whom you witness to share what they make of all this—what they find off-putting, confusing or inspiring. Depending on where they are in their journey toward Christ, you could invite them go with you to a study group designed for people who have questions about God and the Bible. You might invite them to sit in on that small group of people you meet with to learn from the Bible and support one another. There might come a day when you ask, "Have you ever asked Jesus to forgive all your sins? Would you like to make a new start today?" But this would likely be far along in the progression on which you or God had been leading that person.

2. Be personal. It is also important to be clear about what it is that you are inviting people to come and see. Sometimes people invite others to come and see their church. They'll talk about what a fabulous facility or range of programs a certain church has. They may extol the opportunity to build one's business network or hear some marvelous music or get some wisdom on life's

tough issues. A healthy church can be valuable in all those ways. But if the invitation is to a human enterprise, it will ultimately disappoint. It is even better to extend an invitation like we find in Psalm 66:5, "Come and see what God has done, his awesome deeds for humankind!" (TNIV). When you testify to the truth of what God has done in your life or nail before others the sins that slay you, when you express grace under pressure or serve the needs of people before your own, you are inviting them to come explore the wonder of what God can do in a human life.

This points us to the second aspect of Jesus' style of invitation. Jesus extended *personal* invitations. He didn't hand people a doctrinal tract. He asked them to come join him at a dinner table. "Here I am!" he said. "I stand at the door and knock. If anyone hears my voice and opens the door, I will come in and eat with that person, and they with me" (Revelation 3:20). Christ's earliest witnesses followed this focus. They invited people not to a particular piety, place, program or process but to a Person. The essence of the gospel for them was not a religion but a magnificent relationship. They said: "Come and see Jesus" (John 1:42, 47; Hebrews 12:2).

Our witness needs to have this focus too. If we are inviting people to a system of beliefs instead of to Someone worth believing in, then we are not offering them the riches God truly offers. If we are inviting them to meet our pastor and not our Master, we're giving them less than the best invitation. Inviting people to church can be a wonderful starting point, but it will be better still if we can make it clear that we're there because we've met God there.

3. Be practical. We forget sometimes that the twelve men with whom Jesus traveled were not yet "saved" in anything like the fullest sense. Jesus was clearly their rabbi, but not yet their Savior or Lord. There was still so much about Jesus and the the kingdom of God they had not taken in. There was a lot they would *never* understand until they actually practiced obedience to his Way. For this reason, a major part of Christ's ministry with the Twelve involved inviting them into kingdom practices as a means of helping them develop kingdom convictions.

For example, Jesus invited his followers to go out into the countryside without a lot of baggage in order to build their trust in God's provision. He invited them to share what little they had with those who had less in order to develop God's compassion within them. Jesus invited them to spend time with outcasts in order to learn the value of people in the sight of God. He invited them to step out of their boat in order to discover the faith that walks on water.

> WHEN WE ARE OPEN TO GO WHEREVER THE HOLY SPIRIT LEADS US, HE WILL USE US TO SHARE THE GREATEST GIFT OF ALL—ETERNAL LIFE THROUGH JESUS CHRIST. AND WHEN HE DOES, WE MAY NEVER KNOW ON THIS SIDE OF ETERNITY HOW MUCH OF A DIFFERENCE WE MADE. BUT SOMEDAY—ON THE OTHER SIDE—WE'LL KNOW IN FULL.
>
> Craig Groeschel

Until we get this order of learning in its proper sequence, we will tend to spend too much time trying to resolve the unbelief of nondisciples through intellectual argument. The invitation Jesus extends, however, is precisely the opposite: "Follow me, and then you'll find reason for faith." In the kingdom of God, progress in faith follows progress in practice. Obedience builds belief. Who do you know whom you might invite to practice the Way of Jesus as a means of meeting the Person of Jesus?

4. Be passionate. The fourth element worth noting about the way Jesus invited people was his passion. There was an urgency and intensity to many of Jesus' invitations. When he met Zacchaeus, for example, Jesus didn't leave his business card, saying, "Feel free to give me a call, if you ever feel like talking." That would have been the right approach if Zacchaeus had been earlier in his spiritual journey. Sensing the tax collector's readiness for more, however, Jesus seized the moment of opportunity. "Zacchaeus," he said, "come down *immediately*. I *must* stay at your house *today*" (Luke 19:5, italics mine). When the Pharisee Nicodemus came to ask Jesus some serious spiritual questions one night, Christ did not beat around the bush. "If you want to enter the kingdom of God, Nick, you *must* be born again" (John 3:1-7, paraphrase). On another occasion, a man responded to Christ's invitation by saying, "'Lord, first let me go and bury my father.' But Jesus told him, 'Follow me, and let the dead bury their own dead'" (Matthew 8:21-22).

Christ was familiar with the human tendency to always have *some* reason for saying, "Not now, Jesus." When Jesus issued this strident invitation to "Repent, for the kingdom of heaven has come near" (Matthew 4:17 TNIV), his urgency was informed by the knowledge that people often procrastinate when it comes to making decisions like this, even though their salvation is at stake.

When my friend invited me out on that blind-date dinner all those years ago, there was an almost ferocious intensity to his words: "I am going to invite you to a dinner with this girl and, please believe me, you don't want to say no." When a bold youth worker urged me take a leap of faith and ask Christ into my heart at age eighteen, there was a similar loving urgency to his tone. Because of the way both of these invitations were put, I *didn't* say no, and was thereby introduced to the two most important relationships of my life.

5. Be polite. At the same time, it is important to notice that the invitations Jesus issued always contained the understanding that people were free to turn down his offer. The Pharisees said no to the invita-

tion of Jesus. The rich young ruler said no to Jesus. Jesus poured inestimable hours into walking with Judas but, in the end, he too said no to the invitation that would have been his salvation. Jesus issued compelling calls and commands, but he always allowed people their free choice (Luke 14:15-24). He was an officer and a gentleman with people and so must we be. We will be bold to "give the reason for the hope that [we] have," but we will "do this with gentleness and respect" (1 Peter 3:15).

6. Be persistent. There is one last aspect of Jesus' style of invitation worth noting: he was remarkably persistent. The massive variety of parables Jesus told in an effort to lead people into the heart of God is one indication of this commitment. It is as if Jesus was thinking, "Okay, so you aren't ready to take a step into the kingdom on this basis; let me issue the invitation in another way." The patient manner with which Jesus endured the slow growth of the twelve people he worked especially hard to reach is another evidence of this persistence. But what a harvest in the end!

Many of the most important harvests require this kind of perseverance. I once heard of a man named Tedd who had been dating Janet for seven years. Every Valentine's Day, Tedd proposed to her and every year Janet said, "No, not yet." Finally, Tedd reached his limit. He bought a ring, took Janet to a romantic restaurant and summoned up his courage for one last try. Another "no" would mean he had to get on with his life without her. Seeing that Janet had a present for him, Tedd decided to hold his proposal until after she made her gift. "What did you bring me?" he asked. She handed him a box the size of a book. He opened the package and slowly peeled away the tissue paper. It was one of those cross-stitch panels that take a very long time to make. Janet had made this one. It simply said, "YES."[1]

The apostle Paul writes, "Let us not become weary in doing good, for at the proper time we will reap a harvest if we do not give up" (Galatians 6:9). Some yeses are in the making much longer than we can see. Some are worth enduring a lot of noes to finally gain.

SHARE THE GREATEST INVITATION

If you have been a witness in the way we've been exploring in this book, a moment will come when the Holy Spirit gives you the sense that someone with whom you've been speaking may be ready to respond to the greatest invitation of all. Let me suggest five commitment-advancing questions you can ask to help that person come home to the love of God.

1. Are you ready? First of all, ask the person if they are ready to begin a new kind of relationship with God. You may want to reiterate at this point the heart that God has for them. God is like the good shepherd, the searching woman and the waiting father in the parables that Jesus told (Luke 15). He yearns so much to find us and restore us to our treasured place in his household. When he finds us, he knocks upon the door of our heart and waits for us to respond to his invitation to come share life with him. He will not break down the door if we don't want this relationship. He waits for us to invite him in (Revelation 3:20). There are many ways of asking someone if they are ready to answer Christ's knock now and welcome him in. Here are some examples:

- Would you like to ask Jesus into your heart?

- Do you want to begin a new life with God?

- Are you ready to say goodbye to who you've been and hello to the person you can be?

- Would you like to be born again?

- Do you want to become a disciple of Jesus?

- Would you like to make certain you've received God's forgiveness and have become a member of his family?[2]

Different questions may be appropriate in different situations. The point is, pick or find some question that draws a clear line on the sidewalk—one that makes it very clear that a personal decision has been set before them—that a step must be taken which signals their willingness to make a decisive change in the nature of their relationship with God.

If the person does not seem ready or declines the invitation, then back off. It will increase the other person's trust in your heart if you are in no way coercive or pushy. Seek to understand what might be holding this person back. Try to help them address these issues as you go forward together. You might even offer to pray with them right then and there, thanking God for their honest seeking, and asking God to help them with whatever makes it feel like it is still not time to go further. Remember, it is the Holy Spirit alone that converts people. The role of a witness is to simply extend invitations.

2. Do you understand the gospel? If the person you are speaking with accepts your invitation to become a disciple, then ask them to put into their own words what they believe they are saying yes to. This is essential. Becoming a disciple of Jesus is not a decision to take lightly. It is more like saying "I do" at a wedding or "I will" when becoming a citizen of a new country. It is crucial that the person you're witnessing to understand that saying yes to Christ is a life-changing choice. If the person cannot seem to describe the *primary* element of the gospel—the means by which someone *gets right with God*—then gently explain it.

There are many ways of doing so. One way is to tell the first part of "the divine news" we examined earlier in this book (*chap. 2*). In the Going Deeper section at the end of this chapter you'll find a list of books that provide other wonderfully helpful analogies and images for describing this most important part of the gospel message. In talking with nondisciples through the years, I have often used an analogy I developed called the "Three Ladders." You'll find it in the appendix at the end of this book.

Whatever particular language or imagery you choose to describe the good news, the key concept is this: Before someone can truly be saved, they must understand something of the depth of their need and the glory of God's amazing grace. It can be as simple as coming to that state of clarity the writer of the famous hymn "Amazing Grace" described as he lay upon his deathbed. When someone asked John Newton, a former slave trader, what was on his mind, Newton (then an Anglican priest) replied: "My memory is nearly gone, but I remember two things: That I am a great sinner and that Christ is a great Savior."[3]

3. Will you pray with me? Assuming the person to whom you are talking has at least this primary dimension of the gospel clearly in view, then invite him or her into a personal conversation with God. Invite them to pray simply with you. Tell them that you are going to start out the prayer and then leave a space for them to tell God out loud what is on their heart. Assure them that they don't have to be religious-sounding or eloquent. God is only interested in the truth of what they feel in their heart. Despite all the formulas or recipes they may have heard, there is no official script for this. The two major themes of their prayer should simply be: "Save me from sin. Lead me in life." (Be my Savior. Be my Lord.)

4. Do you realize what just happened? Once you've prayed like this, invite him or her to think about what just happened. I sometimes ask people: "Do you feel any different?" People will often say, "I feel like this huge weight has been lifted from me," or "I feel really happy," or "I'm feeling amazed." Sometimes they'll say, "I don't know what to feel," or "I don't feel any different yet." Whatever the response you get, assure the person that their condition before God *has* changed. The Bible teaches that "if we claim to be without sin, we deceive ourselves and the truth is not in us. [But] if we confess our sins, he is faithful and just and will forgive us our sins and purify us from all unrighteousness" (1 John 1:8-9). Tell the person: "You can be absolutely certain that your relationship with God has been put right now. The Bible says that 'if anyone is in Christ, he is a new creation; the old has gone, the new has come!'" (2 Corinthians 5:17).

I will frequently give the person a hug or a handclasp and tell them how thrilled I feel for him or her. "Never forget this day. It's your spiritual birthday!" You might go on to tell them a bit more about the rest of the good news: Because they have a renewed relationship with God, the process of total salvation has begun to unfold. As they tend to their connection with him, God will give them power to start overcoming their character flaws. As they study his Word, he will help them to set their course in life by his reliable truth. He will guide them to participate in his redemptive work in the world. They will enjoy life beyond the grave. He will lead them to become more loving than they were before, and one day he will transform them into a perfectly loving being. This process began when they accepted the in-

vitation of Jesus to be his disciple.

5. Can I help you walk from here? Finally, be sure to issue this invitation, as well. Ask the person if he or she will let you assist them in taking the next important steps. When their prayer for salvation is real, people always accept this offer. We'll explore in much greater depth in the final chapter of this book what this kind of supportive companionship looks like. The key idea is for you to let the person know that you would count it a privilege to be an ongoing resource for them as they take their next steps on the great adventure of discipleship.

BY A BRIGHTER LIGHT

Many years ago, a disheveled man standing 6'6" tall walked off the street into a meeting I was leading at a church near San Francisco. He asked if he could speak to a pastor. Assuming he was looking for a handout, I tried to offer him some money. But the man made it clear that he wanted something better than money. He knew he needed Jesus at the center of his life. Humiliated by my stupidity, I asked him to forgive me, and then sat down with him and went through the kind of process with him that I've described in this chapter. When we were finished, we rejoiced together over the new life he had just begun.

I invited the man, whom I'll call Jerry, to attend our church and gave him a book for new Christians. When he went through some further hard times, I helped him out financially. It was hard for Jerry to find his way fully into the new life. He'd been the child of a prostitute and struggled with alcoholism for many years. There were some deep wounds. Eventually, Jerry lost his way again and wound up back in prison. I wrote letters to him there and saw him once more when he got out. But then I moved away to another part of the state and lost touch completely.

Years later, I came back to the Bay Area and spoke at a midday gathering at a local church. My topic was the outreaching love of God, as displayed in the wonderful parable of the Good Samaritan (Luke 10:25-37). About ten minutes into the discussion afterward, a man toward the back raised his hand and started to speak. The rear of the hall was mostly glass. The morning light streaming through it made it hard to see more than the man's silhouette.

"God once met me when I was in a ditch like that guy in the parable," the stranger said. "One of his servants found me there and helped me up. I wish I could say my life turned around immediately, but it didn't. I wound up in a ditch more than a few times after. But Jesus had his hand on

me and didn't let go. A lot of years have gone by now. I'm finally clean and sober. I've got a good job, a wonderful wife and a pretty fine church."

Something about the voice was eerily familiar, but I couldn't quite place it. The man stepped out into the aisle and began to walk forward. He was neatly dressed, clean-shaven and unusually *tall*. "I wonder if you might remember me," he said. And, suddenly, I did. "Jerry!"

There will come a day when you find yourself in heaven. The glory of God will be streaming everywhere, bathing all you see in a perfectly marvelous light. A silhouette will come walking toward you. You will behold the radiant face of someone who would not be there had you not been a witness. He or she will say, "I wonder if you remember me?" You will gasp with joy and speak their name. And that person will say, "Thank you so much for issuing God's invitation to me. Because of Christ who worked through you, I finally said yes!"

---

[1]A story told at Janet's funeral after seventeen years of marriage to Tedd Rubel Shelly, Nashville, TN.
[2]Bill Hybels and Mark Mittelberg, *Becoming a Contagious Christian* (Grand Rapids: Zondervan, 1994), p. 186.
[3]Jonathan Aitken, *John Newton: From Disgrace to Amazing Grace* (Wheaton, IL: Crossway Books, 2007), p. 347.

Application Exercise

1. Which of the six elements of Jesus' style of invitation do you feel best characterizes your approach to helping other people move further in their spiritual journey?

   ☐ Progressive: I issue progressively deeper invitations in conversation with nondisciples.

   ☐ Personal: I make it clear that I want people to discover a relationship, not a religion.

   ☐ Practical: I invite people to come practice the Way of Jesus with me.

   ☐ Passionate: I communicate with some intensity the value of a relationship with Christ.

   ☐ Polite: I try to be very considerate, giving people freedom to say no.

   ☐ Persistent: I don't give up in the face of a few noes.

2. Read through the list above once more and *underline* the element of Christ's invitational style that you feel you are weakest in. Why do you think this is so?

3. List below the five questions the reading recommends as means of sharing the invitation to salvation. How might you learn these questions by heart so that you'll always be ready to help someone with this kind of process?

4. Look back at the list of people you wrote down in the Application Exercise for chapter six. Might any of these people be ready for you to share the greatest invitation with them? Who else comes to mind?

5. Describe in your own words below the primary element of the gospel—the means by which someone gets right with God. Close your eyes and consider this element for a few moments. Describe what goes through your mind as you consider the element, or draw any images that come to mind.

6. Does the reading convict, challenge or comfort you? Why?

Going Deeper

Choung, James. *True Story: A Christianity Worth Believing In*. Downers Grove, IL: Inter-Varsity Press, 2008.

Hybels, Bill, and Mark Mittelberg. *Becoming a Contagious Christian*. Grand Rapids: Zondervan, 1994.

McLaren, Brian D. *More Ready Than You Realize: Evangelism As Dance in the Postmodern Matrix*. Grand Rapids: Zondervan, 2002.

12 / Point Out the Pathway

LOOKING AHEAD

MEMORY VERSE: Ephesians 4:14-15
BIBLE STUDY: Acts 2:42-47
READING: The Great Imperatives

 Core Truth

What is our responsibility after someone we know has invited Christ into their life?

Our final work as a witness is not leading someone to make the decision to ask Christ into his or her heart, but guiding that person into the life of Christian discipleship. This way of living involves an ongoing journey toward maturity that is marked by several basic commitments needed to discover more of God, to nurture a more Christlike character and to act in the power of the Holy Spirit.

1. Identify key words or phrases in the question and answer above, and state their meaning in your own words.

2. Restate the core truth in your own words.

3. What questions or issues does the core truth raise for you?

Memory Verse Study Guide

Copy the entire text here:

_____

_____

_____

_____

_____

_____

_____

_____

_____

_____

_____

_____

_____

_____

_____

_____

_____

_____

_____

_____

Memory Verse: Ephesians 4:14-15

Of all the disciple-makers we meet in the New Testament none, other than Jesus himself, displays a zeal for helping people all the way home like the apostle Paul. In this passage Paul issues a passionate imperative that should guide the ambition of any new disciple as well as the more seasoned ones who care for them.

1. *Putting it in context:* Our memory verse is set within a chapter that is devoted to describing the nature of the new life believers are meant to have in Christ. *Read Ephesians 4.* What seems to be the "big idea" of this chapter?

2. What are the chief dangers that confront people when they are spiritual "infants" as Paul describes it (v. 14)?

3. Conversely, in what terms does Paul define "maturity" (vv. 13, 15)?

4. What are some of the characteristics of the body of Christ to which believers belong (v. 16)?

5. *Review Ephesians 4:17-32*. What are disciples specifically called to "put away" (vv. 22, 25) as they "grow up" (v. 15)?

6. What does Paul call disciples to do or put on? List as many as you can find in these verses.

7. What do you think would be the effect on this world if every Christian disciple exhibited mature qualities and behaviors like the ones that Paul urges here?

Inductive Bible Study Guide

Bible Study: Acts 2:42-47

In this passage, we are given the first video clip of the early church, following the day of Pentecost and the Spirit-powered outreach of Christ's witnesses. Note the basic elements of the ongoing life of discipleship into which the new believers have entered. This is the life into which we must help new disciples find their way so that they can become mature believers and witnesses themselves.

1. We are told that the new believers "devoted themselves to the apostles' teaching" (v. 42). Why do you suppose this practice was so important for them?

2. The first disciples also "devoted themselves . . . to the fellowship" (v. 42), and "every day they continued to meet together in the temple courts. They broke bread in their homes and ate together with glad and sincere hearts" (v. 46). What might have been some of the benefits of this regular experience of community?

3. Acts reports that the new believers were furthermore "devoted . . . to the breaking of bread and to prayer" (v. 42). "Everyone was filled with awe, and many wonders and miraculous signs were done" (v. 43). They enjoyed praising God (v. 47). How would these experiences have helped develop these new disciples?

4. What orientation toward personal "possessions and goods" do you see described in the life of the early church (vv. 44-45)?

5. Where do you see any of these basic commitments and experiences (questions 1-4) still being practiced by followers of Jesus today?

6. What does the close of the passage say about the *influence* of this lifestyle on the world of nondisciples around them (v. 47)?

7. What questions or issues does this passage raise for you?

Reading: The Great Imperatives

CARING FOR NEWBORNS

Most of us know that the first few moments after a child has been born are particularly critical ones. The child comes out and everyone cheers. But birthing, in the fullest sense, really isn't finished yet. Doctors often need to give babies a gentle slap or clear out their airway so they can begin breathing on their own. A newborn child needs to be put into the mother's arms in order to learn how to nurse. Babies need to be encouraged to move and stretch as well, so that blood will flow freely, allowing the child to truly thrive. Without these vital measures, all the joy that accompanies a new birth may turn to sadness.

If I had been left on my own after my new birth as a Christian, my faith would likely have ended. Being a new believer alone at an Ivy League school isn't much better than being a newborn left on a hillside in winter. I faded quickly. Thankfully, one of the Great Physician's assistants saw my need. An upperclassman named Mark found out that I was a new Christian. "Are you involved in a fellowship?" he asked. I said something about being very busy. Mark didn't buy it. "You better do something or this environment's going to kill you, Dan." His words stung like a slap, but they did the trick. They forced me to draw God's Spirit into my lungs.

"What do you do?" I asked him. He told me about one of the Christian fellowships on campus and said he'd be coming by my room on Friday night to pick me up and take me there. I was stunned, but I agreed to go. "I lead a Bible study in my room on Wednesday nights too," said Mark. "You don't need to be an expert; you just need to be hungry. You're invited to that too." It was the consistent care I needed to survive the neonatal period of my faith and move toward maturity.

You can provide this kind of nurturing care for someone. The first question that needs to seize your imagination after someone has made a decision for Christ is,

> THE PRIMARY GOAL OF SPIRITUAL LIFE IS HUMAN TRANSFORMATION. IT IS NOT MAKING SURE PEOPLE KNOW WHERE THEY ARE GOING AFTER THEY DIE, OR HELPING THEM HAVE A RICH INTERIOR LIFE, OR SEEING THAT THEY HAVE LOTS OF INFORMATION ABOUT THE BIBLE, ALTHOUGH THESE [ARE] GOOD THINGS. LET'S PUT FIRST THINGS FIRST. THE FIRST GOAL OF SPIRITUAL LIFE IS THE RECLAMATION OF THE HUMAN RACE.
>
> John Ortberg

"How can I help this person develop as a disciple of Christ?" Without this aid, that individual will likely drift away from Christ as surely as I would have if Mark had not given me guidance. With your assistance, however, God can take that newborn and help him or her mature into a radiant witness that leads others to him.

THE DNA OF DISCIPLESHIP

So, how do you help someone to develop as a disciple? This chapter's Bible study on the lifestyle of the first disciples illuminates some of the key ingredients (Acts 2:42-47). One way of putting it all together is to borrow an image from the organic world. We know that our physical life develops according to a pattern set by the DNA in our cells. DNA serves as the blueprint for the development and function of our bodies. Each DNA molecule contains a set of *four* nucleotide bases that encode the information that gives each molecule its unique properties and potentiality.

A study of the Scriptures and of common experience suggests that there is a kind of DNA to the spiritual life too, one that is made up of certain important bases. I don't want to stretch this analogy too far, but think of maturation as a disciple as a process of progressively *Discovering, Nurturing* and *Acting*, with each of these movements made up of four basic elements. This portion of the book is written so that you could share it with a new disciple you know.

DISCOVER GOD (WORSHIP!)

Have you ever fallen deeply in love? You couldn't wait to be with that person again. You wanted to know your beloved at every level possible and to be known in such depth and detail too. Or have you ever held a baby in your arms and felt an almost indescribable pleasure in that? You could spend hours studying those tiny fingers and eyelashes, exulting in every sweet breath and squeak. Have you ever felt a thrill of joy when you moved into a new city or house, or began a new video game or project? You become almost obsessed with exploring more and more of that undiscovered territory.

This nearly overwhelming desire to be *with* and *for* someone or something in which you find mystery and meaning is close to what the Bible calls "worship." The Bible teaches that we are meant to find joy in other human beings and pleasure in created things, but to reserve our ultimate devotion, our true worship, for God alone. God's first commandment is to worship him and him alone (Exodus 20:1-6). He issues this commandment not because *he* is insecure but in order to secure *us*. God knows that only through communion with him do we find what we need to make the most of this life (Psalm 100). As the Westminster Shorter Catechism puts it: "The chief end [purpose] of humanity is to glorify God and enjoy him forever."

The call to worship God is, therefore, the first imperative of discipleship. Recounting the calling of the first disciples, the Bible says, "Jesus went up on a mountainside and called to him those he wanted, and they came to him. He appointed twelve . . . that they might be with him" (Mark 3:13-14). Before he ever calls his disciples to *do* anything, Christ simply wants his disciples to be with him. He knows that all meaningful *doing* flows out of this marvelous *being*.

William Temple, the former Archbishop of the Anglican church, writes:

> Worship is the submission of our nature to God's being; the quickening of our conscience by his holiness; the nourishment of our mind with his truth; the purifying of our imagination by his beauty; the opening of our heart to his love; the surrender of our will to his purpose; and all of this, gathered up in adoration, the most selfless emotion of which our nature is capable.[1]

In worship, we enter into the most important discovery process in all of life. In our sitting and listening, in our singing and praying, in our study and our silence, we are seeking to meet the glorious face, the brilliant wisdom, the splendid companionship of God. As we gather regularly with other believers to experience and enjoy God, we also develop a greater capacity to recognize and respond to God wherever we go during the week. Going to a *house* of worship someplace helps us develop a *heart* of worship that we take everywhere we go.

One of the first things a new disciple needs to find is a regular context for wor-

ship with other disciples. You want to enter into the life of meeting together in the temple courts, being filled with awe, and praising God that marked the life of the earliest disciples (Acts 2:42-47). Look for a church or Christian fellowship whose worship life includes the following four bases. The acronym "SEEK" may help you remember these four bases.

Spiritual authenticity. A very important word of caution: Christian worship is not a consumer event but a communion experience. The primary goal of worship is not to be educated or entertained but to be engrafted into God's life in a deeper way. If you come out of a worship service asking yourself, "What did I *get* from that?" you may have brought the wrong attitude with you. Much better questions are: What praise or part of myself was I able to *give* to God? What encouragement was I able to *give* to others there? At the same time, worship needs to be spiritually authentic to you. You must be able to connect on a soul-level with the worship leaders there, the style of music, the content of the prayers or other elements of the service. Give it some time. No worship experience will connect in every way, every week. If, after a season, you sense that you are somehow not able to authentically encounter God in this place, then you may eventually need to find a different worship context. Communion with God is everything for a disciple.

Engaging Bible messages. Look for a worshiping community where (1) the teacher or preacher truly engages the content of the Bible, and (2) the content of the Bible truly engages daily life. Again, don't demand perfection here. Every communicator has some bad days and *you* won't always know what those are. The message that misses you may be exactly the one that the person behind you needed to hear. If you want to mature as a disciple, however, it is essential that you are fed from God's Word. You need to hear God's voice and learn how his grace and truth speak to the questions and concerns of daily life. If this isn't happening, humbly share your hunger with the person preaching. It will help him or her remember what people most need, and maybe they can direct you to resources or others in the church from whom you might learn.

Exalting music and liturgy. The music you sing or hear sung and played in worship is intended to exalt God and express his glorious worth (worship = worthship). It's okay if not every tune makes your spirit soar or sets your foot to tapping. Remember that person behind you. Meditate on the words and let what they or you are saying shape your orientation toward God. The other elements of worship are like this too. The celebration of the sacraments, prayers, creeds, responsive readings and so forth are also powerful ways of discovering more of God and offering more of yourself to him. God will mature you and draw you to himself through all of these worship vehicles. Stay open to

> NOW, WITH GOD'S HELP,
>
> I SHALL BECOME MYSELF.
>
> Søren Kierkegaard

them. Be a communer, not a consumer.

Kingdom milestones. Most churches will include in their worship life some milestones to mark people's progress into or through the kingdom of God. There will be invitations to decision or commitment, dedications and baptisms, testimonies of God's life-changing work in someone, confirmations or commissionings, weddings and funerals, and sacred thresholds of other kinds. All of these are forms of worship as well. They are opportunities for you and others to celebrate the great truths of our faith and the God who leads us forward *to* life, *in* life and *beyond* this life. Pray for those nondisciples in the crowd at these celebrations who may become inspired there to pursue the path of God's kingdom too.

NURTURE A CHRISTLIKE CHARACTER (GROW!)

Now and then, we meet a follower of Christ whose life seems so beautiful, good or strong that it grabs our attention. Perhaps they walk with people in an exceptionally loving manner. Maybe they testify to God's influence on their life or the case for believing in him in very winsome ways. You may be struck by how humbly and honestly they nail the sins with which they struggle or exhibit an unusual grace when under pressure. Perhaps you notice how readily they serve the needs of others or are comfortable sharing invitations for others to come closer to God.

Maybe you've wondered: *Could I ever become like that?* The answer is yes. Jesus said, "Anyone who has faith in me will do what I have been doing. . . . The Holy Spirit, whom the Father will send in my name, will teach you all things. . . . He will bring glory to me by taking from what is mine and making it known to you" (John 14:12, 26; 16:14). The apostle James wrote that God wants to make every disciple "mature and complete, not lacking anything" (James 1:4). "Then," says Paul, "we will *no* longer be infants, tossed back and forth by the waves, and blown here and there by every wind. . . . Instead, speaking the truth in love, we will in all things grow up into him who is the Head, that is, Christ" (Ephesians 4:14-15).

This is why the important question is not *"Could* I ever become like Jesus and his most radiant witnesses?" but *"How* could I become like that?" Amy Carmichael, the great missionary to India, once spoke on this subject:

Sometimes when we read the words of those who have been more than conquerors, we feel almost despondent. I feel that I shall never be like that. But they won through step by step: by little bits of will; little denials of self; little inward victories; by faithfulness in very little things. They became what they are. No one sees these little hidden steps. They only see the accomplishment, but even so those small steps were taken. There is no sudden triumph, no spir-

itual maturity. That is the work of the moment.[2]

God can grow in any of us a substantially more Christlike character, but it requires a willingness to go on a long journey, the *basic* elements of which are the following "STEPs."

Sight for the pathway. The first thing you need to grow is a *vision* of what you could become. God's desire is to make you much more like Jesus by the end of your life's journey than you are today.[3] So set your sights on becoming someone whose life is filled with the love, joy, peace, patience, kindness, goodness, faithfulness, gentleness and self control that we see in Christ (Galatians 5:22-23). The eighteenth-century sage William Law once wrote, "If you stop and ask yourself why you are not as [mature as] the [early] Christians were, your own heart will tell you that it is neither through ignorance nor inability, but purely because you never thoroughly intended it."[4] In other words, it is not enough simply to wish to be like Jesus. You must plan to actively pursue the following practical *means* to that end.

Training for the soul. When we examine the life of the early disciples we are told that they devoted themselves to prayer (Acts 2:42). This is only a hint at the very rich range of spiritual disciplines that the most vital disciples have sown into their daily practice. Resolve that you will not be dependent for your growth on how good a pastor's sermons or teacher's classes are. Supplement whatever pastoral teaching you get with some spiritual practices that can nurture your connection with Christ when you are not in the company of the worshiping community. Ask your Christian mentors to suggest some soul-training exercises or resources (see the "Going Deeper" section at the end of chap. 8). Experiment with a lot of these exercises over time. Like an athlete in daily training, you will grow stronger.

Equipment for life. Third, enroll yourself in some continuing education. We're told that the members of the early church "devoted themselves to the apostles' *teaching*" (Acts 2:42). The picture is of a people who kept pursuing a deeper and deeper understanding of God's Word. Make this your practice too. Read the New Testament on your own. Get into a Bible study someplace. Go to a seminar or class series offered at your church or another one. Ask a mature disciple for some book recommendations. Learn some new mental models and skill sets that will help you live in a more Christlike way in your home, workplace and social circles. Get equipped for your life as a witness (2 Timothy 3:16-17).

Partners for the journey. Jesus once said, "Where two or three come together in my name, there am I with them" (Matthew 18:20). The early Christians took this statement seriously. They "devoted themselves . . . to the *fellowship*. . . . They continued to meet together. . . . They broke bread in their homes and ate together with glad and sincere hearts" (Acts 2:42, 46). The principle here is that disciples grow best in groups. So join a fellow-

ship or small group at a church nearby. Grab some disciples you like and form a group if there isn't such a ministry there. Look for all the Bible verses that talk about how Christ's followers are to treat one another and practice these things with some fellow seekers.

A group of tourists passing through a quaint village came upon an old man sitting beside a fence. One tourist asked, "Were any great men born in this village?" The old man replied, "Nope, only babies." The same must be said for the Christian life. All of us start small, but we are never too old to grow up. If you are willing to nurture your connection with Christ in these intentional, practical ways, you are going to be amazed by how much bigger, better and more beautiful Jesus helps your character become.

ACT IN THE POWER OF THE SPIRIT (SERVE!)

One of the most powerful people I know is a woman who stands just 5'4" tall and speaks with a voice so quiet you often have to strain to hear her. The child of a wealthy physician, Maggie Gobran grew up in the lap of luxury. She attended elite schools, married a prominent businessman, drove a Mercedes and taught at one of Cairo's leading universities. Because her parents were Christians, Maggie discovered much about God through the worship services her family regularly attended. In all of the ways I've described, she nurtured a fine character that many admired. One day, however, Maggie had an experience that would propel her knowledge of God and her likeness to Christ to a whole new level.

Following the death of an aunt who'd made a lifelong habit of serving the poor, Maggie felt moved to go visit one of the slums that house the garbage-pickers of Cairo. She walked for the first time among the stinking piles of refuse and homes made of cardboard and tin that were the estate of the poorest of Egypt's poor. She met children the same age as her own, only these had no shoes or clean clothes, no medical care or schools, no relief from the flies and the sweltering heat, and no prospect of anything ever changing.

Maggie went home that night to her comfortable world, but the experience she'd had unlocked something in her. "How can I know God and claim a character like Jesus and not *act* in some way to address these needs?" She began returning to the slum each day while her kids were in school. She did the little things she could—giving money to get a mother some medical attention, teaching basic lessons on hygiene, math skills and Scripture, washing and bandaging the dirty, scarred feet of children. In time other people began joining her in the work.

Today "Mama Maggie" guides a thousand workers in ministering to some ten thousand poor families. Her ministry (Stephen's Children) has opened dozens of schools and healthcare facilities and a Christian camp where kids go each summer. Nominated for the Nobel Peace Prize, she is often called the Mother Teresa of

Cairo. I know her well enough to be certain that she cares little for this. Her joy is in knowing that a few more children are going to bed with their feet clean, their stomachs full, their hope for the future alive.

What happens to a lake that has no outlet? It stagnates. What happens to a disciple who knows God and grows in Christ but doesn't get around to pouring themselves out in his name? The same thing. This is why Christian service is so essential to a new disciple's life. The basic elements of this part of the DNA of discipleship can be described by the acronym "SERV."

Strategic giving. To be an active servant of Jesus is to be a faithful steward. It is to understand that all of your resources came from God and have been entrusted to you to use wisely and well to advance the Master's kingdom (Matthew 25:14-30). This does not require a vow of poverty. The first disciples apparently had many "possessions and goods." But they were willing to sell them as necessary in order to "give to anyone who had need" (Acts 2:45). Start moving toward the biblical standard of setting aside ten percent of your income (a tithe) for the work of God's kingdom through your local church (Malachi 3:6-12). This is strategic stewardship in two ways: (1) It supplies the monies needed for the uniquely important work your church does in making disciples; and (2) It trains you to prioritize God's concerns in your life (Matthew 6:19-21). Anything you give beyond your tithe to other kingdom work is considered an offering.

External engagements. Second, expect Christ to call you into engagements with the needs of people beyond your normal comfort zone. Jesus routinely did this with the first disciples. He took them into Samaria, a particularly rough neighborhood for Jews, in order to show them needs he longed to meet there (John 4). He called them into conversation with people of other races and cultures to expand their vision of where God was at work (Matthew 8:5-10; Mark 7:24-30). He sent them out on short-term mission trips to address spiritual, medical and material needs (Mark 3:13-15; Luke 9:1-6, 12-17). Jesus even called his disciples to the extremely daunting task of serving their enemies (Luke 6:27-36). Christ will do the same with you. If you respond to his call, he will use these experiences to expand your vision, faith, heart and influence.

Redemptive relationships. Third, recognize that Jesus wants you to build relationships with other people that can further his redeeming work in them. Don't settle into just hanging out with the put-together or Christian people you know. Dare to come alongside people at points of painful loss, crisis or transition in their lives and help them find the redeeming grace and truth of God. Treasure the relationships you have with nondisciples and seek to be a witness who helps them draw closer with God. The Bible says that because of the servant-heartedness the first disciples showed toward the least, the last and the lost, the church "[enjoyed] the favor of all the people. And the Lord added

to their number daily those who were being saved" (Acts 2:47). Someone was a witness to you. Help someone else find his or her way home to the heart of God.

Volunteer ministry. Finally, please see how much your time and talents are needed by your local church. The book of Acts says of the early church: "All the believers were together and had everything in common" (Acts 2:44). The picture is of a community of faith where everyone brought what they had to serve the common good. Your local church may not actually fall apart, but it will certainly fall far short of its full potential for good without the ministry gifts that you and others bring. Even if you are a brand-new disciple or church member, get involved in a volunteer ministry. Let people know what you're skilled in or passionate about, but above all ask where the current needs really are. Picking up a broom is no one's dream job, but then neither is picking up a cross. Sometimes, however, voluntarily walking into a place where garbage and human need is piled high is the next great turning point in God's amazing plan.

You don't have to serve in exactly the way that Maggie Gobran did. You won't have to serve in the ultimate way that Jesus did. But if the basic elements of SERVice we see in their lives and those original disciples aren't visible in *some* way in your life, then you will not mature fully. Don't miss the chance to discover God even more deeply, to nurture a Christlike character even more completely and to act as a conduit of the Holy Spirit even more powerfully. Resolve that you will worship, grow and serve in the basic ways we've explored and do so in a continuing cycle. These are the three great imperatives of a Christian disciple's life.

YOU SHALL BE MY WITNESSES .

Be assured that the God who once brought forth this world as a garden (Genesis 1) is even now moving through history, preparing to return it to that state for which he created it (Revelation 22). In the midst of it all stands a cross and those who know its glory. To those who bear this knowledge he has given a wonderful charge: "You will be my witnesses in Jerusalem, and in all Judea and Samaria, and to the ends of the earth" (Acts 1:8). Answering that call, Christ's witnesses went out from their homes to deliver the gospel to those who would hear. In A.D. 129 a man named Quadratus wrote a letter to his friend Diognetus describing his encounter with this people:

> They cannot be distinguished from the rest of the human race by country or language. Yet, although they follow the customs of the country in clothing, food, and other matters of daily living, at the same time they

give proof of the admittedly *extraordinary* constitution of their own commonwealth. They busy themselves on earth, but their citizenship is in heaven. They obey the established laws, but in their own lives they go far beyond what the laws require. They are poor, and yet they make many rich. They are completely destitute, and yet they enjoy complete abundance. When they are affronted, they still pay due respect. To put it simply, Diognetus: *What the soul is in the body, that Christians are in the world.* It is to no less a post than this that God has ordained them, and they dare not try to evade it.[5]

Will the same be said of us, as it has been said of the faithful down the long cascade of centuries? I hope and pray that it will. For this is the enduring truth: The gospel is *still* the "power of God for the salvation of everyone who believes: first for the Jew, then for the Gentile" (Romans 1:16), then for you and me and those who will come to believe because we have dared to be what this world most needs— witnesses of the life-changing love of Jesus Christ.

Let that adventure go on!

---

[1]William Temple, *Readings in St. John's Gospel* (London: Macmillan, 1940), p. 68.

[2]As quoted by Tim Hansel, *Holy Sweat: The Remarkable Things Ordinary People Can Do* (Nashville: Thomas Nelson, 1989), p. 130.

[3]I am indebted to Dallas Willard for his understanding of the extent to which spiritual growth requires vision, intention and means.

[4]*The Works of William Law, Volume IV* (Eugene, OR: Wipf and Stock, 2001), p. 16.

[5]"The Letter to Diognetus," *Library of Christian Classics: Volume 1* (New York: Touchstone, 1996), pp. 216-18, italic added.

➔ Application Exercise

1. Complete this sentence: "I can help a new disciple by . . ."

2. What are the three major spiritual movements that constitute the DNA of Discipleship?

3. What can you tell a new follower of Jesus to SEEK in a regular worship experience?

4. What does a new believer need in order to STEP forward in their growth?

5. What can you call a new disciple to pursue in order to SERVE Christ in the church and world?

6. You have been ordained to be one of the witnesses Jesus uses to bring his life-changing love to this world.

   a. How has your understanding of what it means to be a *witness* altered as the result of reading this book?

   b. How has your understanding of what it means to be a *disciple* changed?

Going Deeper

Ogden, Greg. *Discipleship Essentials: A Guide to Building Your Life in Christ.* Exp. ed. Downers Grove, IL: InterVarsity Press, 2007.
———. *The Essential Commandment.* Downers Grove, IL: InterVarsity Press, 2011.

Appendix

THE THREE LADDERS

Every person lives their life traveling the rungs of one kind of ladder or another.

THE CIRCULAR LADDER

Some people's journey is like an aluminum ladder that lies on the ground, bent into a circle like a child's first train-track set. In the middle of the circle sits their *self*. For them, there is no greater goodness than having themselves at the center. There is no higher standard or divine accountability. Their journey in life is not aimed "upward" in any ultimate sense. Such people look at human beings as the highest consciousness yet discovered or simply as "gods" who sometimes struggle with a self-image problem. The secular version of this view holds that our "salvation" lies in realizing the evolvable goodness of humanity. Another version sees salvation in awaking to the hidden "godness" of the *human self*. And so around and around *themselves* they go, traveling the track of experimentation, education or enlightenment. For such people, salvation lies in getting a happier and more hopeful view of the glorious power of the human self.

THE CLIMBABLE LADDER

There are others whose view of the spiritual journey is much more vertical. It is like a ladder that stretches from the earth to the clouds. At the bottom of the ladder stands humanity. In the clouds sits God holding in his hand a sack of rewards that constitute "salvation." Maybe this sack contains ultimate knowledge or eternal health and wealth. Perhaps it contains seventy-two virgins, or perfect bliss, or some other prize. The ladder that leads to this reward is a tall one indeed. But those who hold this view contend that if you're will-ing to exert the effort the ladder is certainly climbable. You can get to God on rungs of good deeds or correct thoughts or religious rituals. Many man-made religions teach this. If you become very busy, very enlightened or very pious, you can climb so high that God will say, "Close enough. Better than many. Congratulations! Take for yourself the prize that you've earned."

THE CHRISTIAN LADDER

The Bible teaches another view. There is, it says, an infinitely great and glorious God. If there were an actual ladder between people and him it would be unimaginably tall. Not even the most saintly one among us could ever get close to him in an entire lifetime of climbing. Yet here is the wonder: While we were still sinners, desperately reaching for the next rung, vainly trying to prove our worth and stepping on others as we fought our way up, God traveled the other direction—he crossed the vast distance from heaven and came down to the very bottom of the ladder (Romans 5:8). There he humbly sacrificed himself to pay the price for all our sinfulness.

Now Christ stands next to us, tapping on our shoulder. "Don't waste your time," he says. "You will never make it on your own effort. You're just damaging yourself and others further." Opening up the sack he holds in his hand, Jesus invites us to look inside. We see there a simple wooden cross—the emblem of his gracious love. We start to realize that the true prize hasn't been what we were selfishly chasing. The great treasure is a relationship of love with God himself. "I am enough for your needs," Jesus says. "My grace is sufficient for you" (2 Corinthians 12:9). "Will you take this by faith?" And some of us reply, "Yes."

We start to relax our white-knuckled grip on the rungs of selfishness. Reaching out, we take his grace by faith in hands that tremble, for letting loose of the ladder we fear that we may fall. But, to our amazement, we find that God's grace bears us upward. From that moment on, any good works, and whatever wisdom or spiritual practices we pursue, are no longer acts of grasping but acts of gratitude. They are not a means of earning God's favor but a way of living out of his favor. Salvation is ours already. Now we begin to live anew. Lifted by his grace, motivated by his love, guided by his truth, we are his disciples (Ephesians 2:1-10).

Which ladder are you traveling?

Additional Resources

The books listed below offer further help in strengthening your capacity to present a credible prosecuting and defending testimony.

Colson, Charles, and Harold Fickett. *The Faith: What Christians Believe, Why They Believe It, and Why It Matters.* Grand Rapids: Zondervan, 2008.

D'Souza, Dinesh. *What's So Great About Christianity?* Washington, D.C.: Regnery, 2007.

Little, Paul E. *Know Why You Believe.* Downers Grove, IL: InterVarsity Press, 2000.

McGrath, Alister, and Joanna Collicutt McGrath. *The Dawkins Delusion? Atheist Fundamentalism and the Denial of the Divine.* Downers Grove, IL: InterVarsity Press, 2007.

Strobel, Lee. *The Case for Christ: A Journalist's Personal Investigation of the Evidence for Jesus.* Grand Rapids: Zondervan, 1998.

———. *The Case for Faith: A Journalist Investigates the Toughest Objections to Christianity.* Grand Rapids: Zondervan, 2000.

Zacharias, Ravi. *Jesus Among Other Gods: The Absolute Claims of the Christian Message.* Nashville: Thomas Nelson, 2000.

About the Author

Daniel Meyer is senior pastor of Christ Church of Oak Brook, a nondenominational Christian congregation located in Chicago's western suburbs. A graduate of Yale University (B.A.) and Princeton (M.Div.) and Fuller (D.Min.) theological seminaries, Dan has also served churches in Northern Ireland, New York, New Jersey and California. His additional experience includes work on an offshore oil rig, in a maximum security prison, on a farm and at IBM's world corporate headquarters.

Dan's messages are aired weekly on television and radio throughout the Chicago area on the *Love Changes Life* program and are frequently featured on PreachingToday.com. He is the on-air host of *Life Focus,* a multiple Emmy Award–winning television news magazine, a trustee of Fuller Seminary and coauthor with Greg Ogden of *Leadership Essentials* (IVP, 2007). Dan and his wife, Amy, make their home in Hinsdale, Illinois, and have three sons.

THE ESSENTIALS SERIES

Discipleship Essentials
Greg Ogden

978-0-8308-1087-1, paperback, 237 pages

Leadership Essentials
Greg Ogden and Daniel Meyer

978-0-8308-1097-0, paperback, 176 pages

Witness Essentials
Daniel Meyer

978-0-8308-1089-5, paperback, 230 pages

The Essential Commandment
Greg Ogden

978-0-8303-1088-8, paperback, 208 pages